Juggling Two Families

Where do I fit in?

Valerie

Contents

Dedication

This book is dedicated, first and foremost, to my mom and dad. They were consistently there to help me out through good times and bad times throughout my whole life. I love you both so very much. You both are the best!!!

My mom, **Lois Hilgendorf**, was always there to lift me up when I was down. When I had a good day, I would call her. When I had a bad day, I would call her. She listened to me and gave me encouragement every time. She accepted me for who I was and always let me know she loved me. Rest in peace, Mom. I love you forever and ever, and I miss you so much!

My Dad, **Marvin VanBrande**, is always there for me no matter what. If I need something, I can call him, and he will show up. He is always ready to help me out in times of need. He truly believed in me more than anyone in my life. He has always told me how proud he is of me and has never failed to let me know how much he loves me. He is the best Dad ever! I love you from the bottom of my heart, Dad!

My support system is my family. I am so lucky to have such a great family, and I dedicate this book to all of you. I love you all so very much!

My husband, **Charles Apsey**, is my rock and gives me strength when I am down.

My son, **Christopher Apsey**, who stole my heart at birth, whom I am so proud of.

My daughter, **Alicia Apsey**, my sweet, precious little girl, whom I am so proud of.

My daughter, **Kenzie Apsey**, who is my baby, I yearn to love and cherish.

My wonderful Grandchildren, I adore each and every one of you

Lola, Liam, Rose, Maple, Ivy, Atlas, and one to come.

My sister, **Angela VanBrande**, who is my very best friend.

My brother, **Marvin VanBrande**, who always had open arms & gave the best hugs.

My brother, **Michael Hilgendorf**, who is the most dedicated person I know.

My brother, **Brent VanBrande**, who has so much ambition and gusto for life.

My Step mom, **Sandy VanBrande**, who has been a major influence in my life.

My Mother in law, **Cherith Staels**, who loves the Lord with all her heart.

My Grandma, **Murl Dowling**, who had so much love to give & always prayed for me.

My Grandma, **Merieda VanBrande**, who fed everyone that walked in her door.

To all of my **nieces and nephews**: There are too many to name, but I love you all!

Acknowledgment

I would like to thank God for giving me the courage and strength to overcome all the obstacles in my life. I have become a better person due to his guidance and love. I pray this book helps children with split families to learn how to cope with the struggles divorce brings into their lives.

I would also like to thank my husband, Charles Apsey for being there for me and having patience with me while I spent hours writing this. He helped me brainstorm and come up with some ideas. He was a big support while I worked on this book.

I would also like to thank my sister, Angela VanBrande, for fully supporting me while I wrote this book. She also helped me brainstorm new ideas and was with me throughout the whole publishing process.

Thank you for supporting me!

I Love you, Charles Apsey and Angela VanBrande!

About the Author

I know the struggles that come with growing up in two families all too well, as I have lived most of my life with divorced parents. I understand the confusion of going back and forth and always feeling like you have to choose one or the other: Mom or Dad.

How can you possibly choose one?

As a preteen, I didn't believe in marriage. My mom and dad were separated when I was three. My Mom and Step Dad were divorced when I was twelve. Being two divorces was enough for me to know that I didn't want to get married.

I met Charles Apsey when I was fourteen. He was also brought up in two families. He knew the struggles of having divorced parents, just like I did. Meeting him made me change my mind about marriage. We were married by the time I turned nineteen. I believe our experience of being raised in split families helped both of us to always work on our relationship and to keep our marriage strong.

We have now been married for 34 wonderful years. Thankfully, my children never had to grow up in a split family.

I wrote this hoping to help at least one child to learn how to cope with life's unpredictable changes. Accept it, and move forward in life. You will feel so much better.

Don't fight what you can't change. You truly can create your own happiness.

Preface

Hi, I am Samantha and I have no idea how to fit in with all of the changes going on in my life. My mom and dad are split up. Mom seems so sad and I miss having dad around all the time. Life is just so different.

If that isn't bad enough, dad goes and finds a girlfriend and moves her into his new house. I only get a small amount of time with him and now I have to share that time with his girlfriend.

Then my mom decides to start dating and gets serious with a man who has kids. To make things worse, his two boys are loud and obnoxious. Now I have all of these new people in my life and I just want things to go back to the way they were. I want it to be just me, mom and dad.

I struggle to fit in as my frustration grows, and mom and dad don't seem to care. I am trying to find my way through it all, but feel so lost. Everytime I start to adjust, something else comes up and more changes come.

My one escape is going to school and seeing my friends. That is the only place I feel normal. It's my safe place, but it seems even this is being jeopardized. I can hardly take all of these changes in my life. I really need to figure this all out before I lose my mind!

I am trying to learn how to deal with everything, but it is all happening too fast. I hope things can slow down a little so I can take it all in and learn how to accept all of these changes.

Chapter One

Mom Life

"Samantha what on earth are you doing? You are supposed to be in school!"

I quickly jerked my head up in surprise. My mother was standing in the doorway, tapping her foot impatiently. I could tell she was very irritated with me by her voice alone. Her facial expression said even more. She was definitely on the verge of anger.

"Oh shoot, not again!" I said as I quickly jumped out of bed and ran to my dresser to find some clothes. I rummaged through my drawers while my mother began to give me another lecture about getting up on time for school.

"Samantha, you are going to have to learn to get yourself up and ready for school. How many times am I going to have to tell you before you start listening to me? You know I have no other choice but to work, and I can't take days off just to make sure you get up for school. The only other solution is to get a babysitter. Then, she could make sure you are up and ready to catch the bus."

I stopped rummaging through my drawer and looked up at mom. I pleaded with her, "No, mom, Please don't get a sitter. I'm old enough to take care of myself. Please, I'm not a baby anymore."

Mom placed her hands on her hips and said, "Well then, start getting up on time for school! This is the last chance you will get, girl! If this happens one more time, I'll get Martha to come over every morning to get you up."

Yuck! Martha? I guess it is time to get serious about waking myself up for school. She is my mom's friend who lives next door. She drives me crazy! All she talks about is men. She is always trying to get mom to go on a date with this one guy. I guess it is her boyfriend's brother. I get so mad at her sometimes. I don't want my mom to date, but Martha is always trying to get her to go out with someone.

My mom and dad just split up about nine months ago. Mom is not ready to go out with anyone, and I don't want her to ever be ready. The two of us are doing just fine. A man can only screw things up on us. Besides, men are gross.

I finally found a decent shirt and my favorite pair of jeans. They have holes in both knees, but they don't bother me. It's my mom that hates them so much.

I put my clothes on the bed and was about to pull off my nightgown when I realized mom was standing there, looking at me. I instantly stopped and looked at her, pleading for her to leave. Being twelve isn't easy, you know.

While most girls have already started to develop, I have just recently started. I was so anxious to be like all the other girls my age that last summer, I started some exercises, hoping they would make me develop faster. Just as I was about to give up, I found two very small mounds on my chest. I was standing in front of my mirror when I discovered them.

I was so excited I ran down the hall and called my best friend, Tricia. I told her about my discovery and we talked excitedly about how I might just catch up to everybody after all. But now we are six months into school, and they still haven't grown much. I am really embarrassed about them, and I won't even let mom in my room when I am getting dressed. Mom understands, thank God. I didn't even have to explain. She just understood without me saying a word.

Mom turned to leave the room, saying, "I will be in the living room waiting for you. Hurry up! I am tired and need to get some rest."

"Okay, mom," I said as I motioned her to go so I could get dressed.

She smiled at me and closed the door behind her. What a great mom. I am so lucky to have her. I hurried along, and soon I was ready to go.

I tried to hide my jeans as I wrapped a sweater around my waist, but it was no use. You can't hide anything from mothers.

She looked over at me and said, "The least you can do is wear decent clothes. Everybody will be looking at you when you walk into class late again!"

I cringed at the thought of everyone staring at me. I hate it when that happens, which is quite often since mom got her new job. Maybe it really is time to start waking up on time.

On the way to school, mom was looking me over. I thought she was going to start lecturing me about my clothes again, but she didn't. She just smiled and turned her attention to the road.

Mom said quietly, "Hunny, I think it might be time to go shopping." What an odd thing to say at a time like this. Besides, money was pretty tight since dad left. "Shopping?" I asked.

Mom smiled and glanced my way. She said, "I don't mean a big shopping spree. I just think it might be time to shop for your first bra."

I about died right then and there! I couldn't believe she brought this up. I was so embarrassed, my face turned bright red.

Mom took notice and spoke up, "You don't have to be embarrassed by this, sweetheart. We have to talk about it sometime. Besides, we can't put it off much longer by the looks of it.

I threw my arms up in the air. "MOM!!" I exclaimed.

I swear my face became fire-red! I cringed as I crossed my arms to cover myself.

I began to stutter, "I know…it's just…well, I felt super excited at first, but now it's…well, just embarrassing."

I felt so stupid. I hate it when I feel inadequate and awkward. Mom pulled up in front of the school and gave me a kiss. She patted my shoulder and said, "We will talk about it more tonight, okay?"

I turned away from her so she couldn't see my red face. I said, "Alright, I love you Mom."

"I love you too, Sam," she called out as I jumped out of the car.

I ran into the school and went straight to class. As usual, everybody turned their heads to stare. Mrs. Windleton was at the blackboard teaching the class. She stopped teaching and gave me a hard look. I wished I could disappear at that moment. I could tell she was irritated. I guess mom wasn't the only one annoyed by me sleeping in frequently.

Mrs Windleton finally said, "Samantha, go wait in the hall. I will be with you in a minute." The whole class started to oooh and aaaah. I was so embarrassed! (as you can see, I get embarrassed a lot) I walked out of the room as fast as I possibly could.

I sat on the floor in the hallway. I knew I was in for it. I was so nervous, and my mind was going over all the things she might say to me. The more I thought about it, the more nervous I became.

Finally, Mrs. Windleton opened the classroom door and came into the hallway. She slowly closed the door and walked toward me. My heart leaped in fear. I stood up and leaned against the wall for support.

Mrs Windleton said, "Samantha, why on earth have you walked into my class late all week? I can understand once in a while, but this has been ongoing. It is very disruptive. Is there a problem I should be aware of?"

I closed my eyes for a second and exhaled. She seemed more concerned than angry. She was actually being halfway decent about the situation. What a relief!

I responded, "Well, my mom started a new job a few weeks ago. She doesn't get home until 8:30 in the morning. I am just not used to waking up by myself, and see, my mom always woke me up before."

Mrs. Wimbledon nodded her head, "Oh, okay. I see, but you have to stop being tardy, or I will have to start giving you detention. I expect you to be here on time from now on. Otherwise, you will have to start sitting in the office until my class is over. Let's get in the classroom. I have a class to teach."

Whew, I was off the hook for now. Next time, I might not be so lucky.

The day ended up turning out pretty good. I got an A on my English test, we had a class discussion on careers and I had the chance to tell Tricia about mom taking me to get a bra soon.

Oh, and today, I finally talked to Jake for the first time! He is the only boy I have ever had a crush on. I still have my doubts because my feelings tell me he will end up as stupid and dumb as any other boy I met; but for now, it is super exciting! He sits next to me in class. He actually asked me if I had a pen he could borrow. I didn't have one, but boy, I wished I did! I can be so unprepared sometimes. I was so glad he at least talked to me, though. It only made my day even better.

On the way home, Tricia and I sat together on the bus and talked about me getting a bra. I finally started to feel like I belonged since I was soon to have a bra of my very own. I will finally be just like the other girls my age. Finally!

The bus pulled up to my driveway, and I ran into the house, anxious to find out if we were going to go shopping.

As I took off my shoes in the entranceway, I heard muffled voices coming from the kitchen. I figured Martha must be here. Mom and Martha were always in the kitchen gossiping about the neighborhood over a cup of hot tea. I hope I never do that when I grow up. It seems boring and dumb. I walked into the kitchen, gave her a hug and proudly handed her my English test. I stood there, waiting for her reaction.

"Oh, good job, Samantha!" mom said as her eyes lit up in joy. She reached over and gave me another hug. I love it when she makes a big deal out of my good grades. No matter how many A's I get, she always makes a big deal out of each and every one of them. I guess she figures it is a strong incentive. She must be right because I am always trying to get good grades just so I can bring them home to show her. Mom looked at Martha and handed the paper to her.

"Samantha has an A," she said proudly.

Martha looked at the paper and sat it on the table as she continued, "Well, that's nice. Oh, Sharon, you'll never believe what happened to me today!"

I slowly faded away from their attention. This was normal whenever Martha was around. She doesn't have kids, so I guess she doesn't understand. She never failed to take mom's attention away from me. I picked up my test and went into my bedroom. I knew my day would only get worse if I stayed in the same room with Martha.

I sat on my bed and read an old Western romance book I found in the den one day. I thought it would pass the time until Martha went home. I hoped she would go home soon so I could spend time with mom and maybe go shopping for a bra with her.

At last, there was a slight rap on my bedroom door. Yay, Martha must have left.

"Samantha," my mom spoke softly.

"Come in," I called as I put the book under my pillow. I wasn't sure if mom would let me read it or not, so I didn't want her to see it. She walked over and sat beside me on the bed.

"Well, are you ready to go shopping for your first bra?" she said as she winked at me.

I smiled big. "Yes!" I exclaimed as I jumped up and headed for my shoes. I didn't even blush this time. I wondered if this was the first step in growing up.

So off we went to find a bra. I felt so grown up! Once we were in the stores, my whole demeanor changed. As mom held bras up to show me, my face began to burn as I looked around to see if anyone could see us. I knew I was beet red from embarrassment. My face burned more and more each time mom held up another bra to show me. There were so many people around, and they all seemed to be watching us.

Getting a new bra seemed like such a private thing and here we were, out in the open, with mom holding up bras in front of me like she was trying to picture it on me. Mom showed no modesty at all and made it very obvious we were bra shopping for me. How embarrassing!

Before long, it was time to go home for supper. I ended up with three bras. I was so glad when we left the store. As I jumped in the car, I felt relieved that it was finally over. Thank God we were on our way home. I really wanted a new bra, but gee whiz, that was embarrassing. I carried the bras on my lap the whole way home. I couldn't wait to get home so I could try them on.

Before long, we were pulling in the driveway. I ran in the house and ran straight to my room. I tried on all three bras, one after another. I inspected each one carefully in the mirror to see if it made a difference. Yes, it did make a difference! Now I can see more curve! I was finally beginning to look like a real woman!

"Samantha, will you come help me with supper?" Mom called.

"Okay, give me just a minute," I hollered as I took one last look in the mirror. I looked back at the bras on my bed, quickly took off my shirt, and threw on the one with the pretty little blue flower in the front. I took one last lingering look and threw on my t-shirt to go and help mom.

We prepared and ate a scrumptious meal with sirloin tip steak, a baked potato, rolls and green bean casserole. It was delicious! We washed dishes together and sat down for a nice, quiet evening of television.

Mom suggested I go to bed early so I can make sure I get up on time for school. I argued that I would have to go to sleep before she even left for work, but she insisted I try it at least for the rest of the week.

As I lay in my bed dozing off, I kept thinking, "Get up to the alarm, get up to the alarm." Guess what? It worked! I was up and ready for the bus. Maybe I really did need more sleep than I thought.

School was alright, except for being a little uncomfortable in my new bra. For some reason, I felt like everybody could see it through my shirt. Plus, the latch jabbed me in the back all day. It started really hurting by the end of the school day. When I got home I checked it out to see why it was bothering me so bad. To my surprise, I had the dumb thing inside out. No wonder it was so hard to get it latched. How stupid of me!

I put my bra on the right way and went to talk to mom. She was outside hanging up laundry on the clothesline. She turned around and saw me coming. She smiled at me and continued hanging up her clothes.

"Hi, hunny, How was school?" mom asked. "Okay," I replied.

"Glad to see you made the bus on time this morning," Mom said. "Yeah, me too," I said proudly.

"Once you get in the habit, you will be fine," mom said, nodding her head.

"Yep," I responded as I thought of Martha. Anything to keep her away.

"So, did you wear your bra to school today?" asked mom with a twinkle in her eye.

"Yep," I answered. I wasn't about to tell her I wore it inside out all day. I felt so grown up and even more confident. Funny how a bra would boost your self-confidence. I wasn't about to tell her this.

She would probably laugh at me or think I was stupid or something.

Mom hung up the last of the laundry, and we walked side by side toward the house.

The rest of the week went great. I felt pretty confident about wearing a bra and Martha didn't come to visit mom.

Friday after school, I packed my clothes for dad's house. I was pretty excited to see him. I missed him so much. When I was finished packing, I went to find mom.

I found her in the flower bed in the backyard. She loved her flowers. She was cleaning out the debris from winter. I bent down and started helping.

"Do you have your clothes packed for your dad's?" she asked as she continued to clean up.

"Yep, I'm done packing. Do you know what time he is coming?" I asked anxiously.

"He said he would try to be here by six o'clock. He has a few errands to run before he picks you up. He thought it would be better to get it all done before he got you so you won't have to be left with Lindy," she responded.

He thought right!

Chapter Two

Dad Life

Lindy is dad's girlfriend. She lives with dad and we don't get along at all. I just don't like her. She is only twenty-one, while my dad is in his thirties. As soon as he moved out of the house, this girl showed up at his new house and never went home. It just wasn't fair to me or mom. I think she might have been the reason he moved out in the first place.

Anyway, the last weekend I was there, dad went away for a few hours and left Lindy and me alone. She was really mean to me and we got into a big fight. She hit me in the head, but I didn't say anything to dad about it and neither did she.

When I went home, I told mom what happened, and boy, was she mad! She ranted and raved for a little while and then called dad. I begged her not to, but she wouldn't listen. She screamed and hollered at him about Lindy and how she was to never touch me again. I could hear dad yelling at Lindy through the phone, too, so I know he was mad as well. I was feeling pretty bad, kind of felt like shrinking down to nothing and disappearing.

Later, I went to my mom and asked her if things were okay between her and dad. She assured me things were okay and that dad was mad at Lindy, not us. I was relieved. I didn't want mom and dad to fight over me. That already happened over custody and I hope to never be the reason for them fighting ever again! It was really bad, and it confused me so much.

"I can't stand her, Mom," I said as I laid my head on her shoulder. She was sitting at the kitchen table at the time.

"Sam, you really need to talk to your dad. If he doesn't know what is going on when he leaves, then how can he fix it?" mom said, trying to sound convincing.

"It's not going to fix anything; all it will do is make things worse," I said defiantly.

Mom sounded more stubborn than ever, "Either you talk to him or I will. This has to stop."

"Okay, I will. But give me some time to think about it," I said. "Okay," mom stood up and kissed me on the forehead.

"It just sucks he had to move her in. It makes me not want to go there anymore," I said as I thought of what it would be like without her there.

Mom put her arms around me and we squeezed each other tight.

"I know, sweety. Just give it some time. You'll see, things will get better." she said as she squeezed me even more. Somehow, I didn't believe that.

Just then, the phone rang. Mom went to answer it and I went to my room, feeling lonely and awkward about things in general. I always feel this way right before I go to dad's house. Lindy makes my life miserable. I wish she would just disappear. I grabbed my book from under my pillow and settled into bed to read. It always takes my mind off things when I am troubled.

Mom popped her head in the door just as I opened my book. "Your father just called. He said he is on his way over. He will be here in about ten minutes."

"What? He said he had things to do before he came," I replied as I jumped up to get ready.

"I guess he must have finished up early," she said and shrugged her shoulders.

"Okay, I will be ready in a minute," I responded.

I put my book in my suitcase and finished packing my stuff. I took my suitcase out to the living room.

Mom asked me if I remembered my deodorant this time. I told her I did. The last time I went to dad's, I forgot to pack it. Dad took me to the store to buy some new deodorant and Lindy was really mad for some reason. I really didn't know what was going on, but they were quietly arguing right before we left. When we came back, she seemed even angrier than before. I don't know why, but I had a feeling it was because of me.

Just as I put my suitcase down by the front door, dad's truck pulled into the driveway. I ran to mom, gave her a hug and kiss goodbye, and out the door I went. Dad got out of the truck and walked over to me. I sat my suitcase down, and he gave me a big hug and kiss. He took my suitcase and put it in the back of the truck. I glanced in the truck to scope out who came with him. There was nobody in the cab. Thank God Lindy didn't come with him. Dad opened the door and patted the seat for me to hop in. He went around to the driver's side, hopped in and shut the door.

"I thought we would go grab some ice cream before we go home," he said as he started the truck.

I looked over at him and smiled big. Ice cream was my favorite! "Sounds great!"

We went to the small ice cream shop just around the corner from where dad lived. I got a giant waffle cone with Superman ice cream and dad got pineapple (YUCK!) ice cream on a regular cone. When we finished eating, we went to the store to get popcorn and candy. Dad decided to make a movie night for us. After getting a bunch of goodies, we went home (I know, it's weird to have two homes).

When we pulled in, of course, Lindy came gallivanting out the door. She can never wait for us to come in. She has to come running out like we have been gone forever or something. It drives me crazy!

"Hey, where have you guys been?" she asked as she put on a fake smile and walked right by me. She put her arms out as she walked toward dad and wrapped her arms around my dad like he was her lifeline or something. She gave him a big kiss and I felt my stomach turn. She is so pathetic!

Dad turned away from her and reached into the back of the pickup to get my suitcase.

"We went to the ice cream place and the grocery store." I piped in, more to remind her of my presence.

Lindy leaned into dad again and gave him another big kiss. It just made me sick so I rolled in my eyes and just walked off into the house. She is so stupid!

Since it was early, we sat down to watch a movie. It was a romance. It was great! I just loved it! It was so romantic at some points. That is how it should be with everybody. Love should stay. It would, if everybody would try. My mom and dad gave up. I don't know why. I wondered if it had anything to do with me.

We made popcorn and settled in to watch another movie. By the end of it, I was lying on the floor, all sprawled out.

After the movie, Dad said, "Well, it's about time we all sit down and have a little talk. Come on up here, Samantha."

I grabbed the pillow I had and slowly got up. I really didn't want to do this. I knew my mom must have told him how bad things really were between me and Lindy. I climbed up on the couch with dad and hoped he would be quick about it. I wanted to become invisible. I didn't want to confront mine and Lindy's problems. I'd rather just let it all slide by and forget about it. I wished I had never said anything to mom. Speaking of mom, I secretly wished I were home with her right now.

Dad put his arm around me and let out a sigh. He began, "I just wanted to tell you that I love the both of you, and I really wish you two would get along. I care about you (he looked at me and gave me a little squeeze), and I care about you (he looked at Lindy and gave her a squeeze). I just can't stand the thought that you don't at least try to like each other." Dad stopped for a minute and rubbed his chin as if in deep thought. I think he was having a real hard time trying to figure out what to say next.

Dad looked at me and said, "Samantha, this is the girl for me. I love Lindy and she is here because I love her. I want you to respect me enough to at least try to get along with her."

Dad stopped and looked at Lindy. "Lindy, this is my daughter. She is my only child and she is very special to me. I wish you would value her as I do and treat her with love and respect."

Both of us hung our heads low in shame as dad continued to pour his heart out to us. By the time it was over, we were both clinging to him and crying. We both apologized for being so mean to each other. Lindy picked her head up off dad's shoulder and looked at me with her red, swollen eyes.

She said, "Let's just forget everything and try to be friends. Is it a deal?" She extended her hand toward me.

I didn't know what to say, so I said, "Okay." We shook hands as if to seal the deal.

By then, it was late and dad tucked me in on the couch. The house he bought was only a one-bedroom. It made me feel like he didn't want me around at first, but he promised me he would add on to the house soon so I could have my own room. It made me feel better to know he was at least thinking of me.

I think all the crying made all of us sleep better that night because we all slept until noon. I guess it was a release from all the pressure of everything for the past nine months or something.

We all woke up and sat at the table together while I drank hot chocolate and they had their coffee. It seemed like we were all more relaxed than normal. (Usually, when Lindy was around, everything seemed more tense.) I actually enjoyed sitting there with them, making small talk. Lindy even asked me about school. She never cared to hear about my life, so it took me by surprise.

Since it was so late, we ate breakfast for lunch. Lindy cooked the eggs and bacon and I made the toast and poured orange juice. It seemed nice to sit together at the table and eat. We never did that before. We always ate at different times and in different rooms. The only thing is, it made me miss mom. She should have been there in Lindy's place. It was all wrong with Lindy there. I looked up at her while my thoughts were running wild, and I saw her winking at my dad as she said something about freshening up. I was overcome with a jealous urge and wanted to say something, but my heart told me to be still. My dad winked back at her. It felt like they were taunting me. I felt like I shouldn't be there.

I was once again out of place in my own dad's house. As always. I quietly slipped out of the kitchen and went to the living room to sit by myself. I really despise the way they pretend I am not there. They just make me feel like I don't belong here. It seems like I am not important anymore because they have each other. I turned the TV on and tuned out my feelings. I don't think they even noticed I left.

I perked up when I heard my dad's voice, "Well, hey, we better get moving if we are going to go." I wondered where we were going.

Lindy jumped up and began to clear the table, while dad jumped in the shower. I was very curious about what we were going to do, so I went to the kitchen to help Lindy clean up. I hoped she might let me in on the plans. Of course, it didn't work, but she sure seemed to appreciate the help.

I thought maybe I should help her more often. It might help us to get along better. Dad came out of the bathroom and went straight to his room. Lindy followed him. There I am, once again, left out in the cold. I was jealous of them being so close. I wanted my dad's attention so badly because I hardly got to see him anymore. I just can't compare to Lindy. Life stinks! I slumped on the couch again and stared blankly at the television.

Dad eventually came out and sat on the couch beside me. "Hey, What's up?" he asked. I shrugged my shoulders and kept my eyes on the television. He kept looking at me like he wanted to say something but didn't have the courage. Finally, he said, "We have a big day planned today." as he turned his attention to the TV.

I looked up at him, wondering if it included me.

He looked at me and said, "We are going to take you to the mall and get you some new shoes and a few pairs of jeans."

I thought maybe my ripped jeans might have something to do with it, but I didn't care. I gave him a big smile and hugged him tight.

As an afterthought, I asked him if Lindy was going. He said yes, which kind of disappointed me. I really didn't want her to go.

"When are we going?" I asked.

He said, "Whenever you are ready."

I jumped up, opened my suitcase and rummaged for some clothes. I got ready as fast as I could. I finally put my shoes on to leave and realized how old and rugged they looked. I didn't realize how bad they were until now.

My day turned out great! I got three new pairs of jeans, a nice pair of Nike's, two shirts and a beautiful necklace. Lindy looked pretty mad when dad offered to buy the necklace for me. It was pretty expensive. I don't think she liked it at all, but I just smiled inside. Hah! She wasn't the only one who got nice things! I felt a bit of triumph for a moment.

It was an awesome day of shopping with dad. There was only one problem: Lindy was there. I tried to pretend she wasn't there but she kept talking to me and asking me questions. I had no choice but to answer her because dad would get mad if I ignored her. I think she knew what I was doing, but I didn't care. I just wanted to enjoy my time with dad.

By 5:00 the next day, I found myself in the truck with dad driving me back to mom's. We pulled into the driveway and mom instantly came out to greet me with a hug and kiss on the forehead. She asked me how my weekend went. I didn't have a chance to answer her because dad came around the truck and handed me my suitcase and shopping bags.

Mom noticed the shopping bags and asked, "What's in the bags?"

Dad told me he loved me, gave me a quick hug and was pulling out of the driveway in a flash. He did his normal beep beep as he drove off. I turned around and waved. When I turned my attention back to mom, she looked irritated for a split second. Then she noticed me looking at her and gave me a big smile. She always looks so pretty when she smiles like that! It never fails to put a smile on my face.

I opened the bags right there in the driveway to show her what dad had bought me. She looked different when I pulled out the jeans and shoes to show her. I have seen this look on her so many times since dad left. She never really says much, but I can tell she isn't happy. I showed her the necklace last. Her eyes were wide at first, then she became sullen, almost angry looking. She told me he shouldn't be buying me things like that. I stopped fiddling with the necklace and looked at her with a puzzled look.

Why shouldn't he? He buys Lindy way more expensive jewelry than this. I didn't get what she meant, but didn't want to continue listening to her. I put my necklace in the bag, picked up all my things and told mom I wanted to go put my stuff away. I walked into the house.

Off I went to my room, still wondering why mom said that. It irritated me that she thought I didn't deserve nice things. I am old enough and I take good care of my stuff, too. I just didn't understand what would be so disturbing about dad buying me a necklace. Lindy gets plenty. Why shouldn't I?

Chapter Three
Mom's Little Chat

That evening, mom pulled out the Monopoly game and we started to play. We always spent the evening together like this when I came home from dads' house. I always looked forward to evenings like these. I just love spending time with mom. Mom was acting differently right from the beginning of the game. I couldn't put a finger on why. She kept looking up at me like she was going to say something, then she would continue the game. She did this enough times that I finally realized something was coming. I just didn't know what.

I wondered if it would be about the necklace dad bought me. I still had no clue why she would be mad at dad for buying me something nice. Why would it bother her so bad? She should be happy for me.

The phone rang a few times and mom answered both calls. She walked away from our game and talked in a very quiet voice for both calls. She didn't say much, but I heard her say "not yet" a few times. I knew that something was going on. I kept waiting for it to come.

Finally, halfway through the game, I stopped playing and asked her, "Is there something you want to say to me?" She looked up at me and then looked down at the board game. Her eyes were darting back and forth and her motions were robotic. She seemed too nervous to really talk. This was not going to be good news.

"Well, uh…yeah… I think it's time we had a little chat," she said as she looked down at the game. She paused a little longer than normal. I perked up, wondering if something was wrong.

She began as she looked up at me with the saddest eyes, "Samantha, I know it has been rough for both of us getting used to your dad not being here. We have had some hard times with me going to work full time. We are finally getting used to our new life…" She paused and fidgeted a bit. She continued, "I've been thinking about things and I think it is time for me to start going out and meeting people. I hope you will be okay with it…."

I didn't know exactly what she was getting at, but I wondered if she meant dating. No, she couldn't mean that because she always said that dad was the only man for her. Dad moved out about nine months ago and mom had spent most of her time crying over him.

She went out and got a job right away since there was no income coming into the house. She took a midnight job so she could still spend evenings with me. Our neighbor, Martha, watched over me for a while.

A few months ago, I begged mom to let me stay by myself. She finally gave in under certain conditions.

For months, my mom just cried all the time. I thought maybe she hated her job, but one day I overheard her talking to Martha about dad, and how heartbroken she was over him. I guess Lindy must have been a big part of the problem since her name came up so often.

Martha always tried to get mom to start dating. She always told her she didn't want to, because dad was the only man she ever wanted to be with.

Besides, having Lindy around was bad enough. What if mom did the same thing and found someone who hated me? I couldn't stand to lose both of my parents. I so wanted it to be just me and mom, and couldn't think of it any other way. The thought of her dating puts my stomach in knots.

I decided just then that mom couldn't mean going out with men. There was just no way she would even think of doing that. She loved my dad way too much.

"Well, where are you going to meet people?" I asked in a matter-of-fact way.

Mom grabbed my hands across the table. She looked me deep in the eyes and said, "Sam, I mean dating. I am going on a date this week."

I was shocked! I didn't know what to say. My thoughts were running wild. I had to take a moment to gather myself together before I could respond. I must have looked pretty silly just staring at her. She left me speechless and dumbfounded. I never in a million years expected this.

Thinking of mom dating made me sick to my stomach. I didn't want her to because I was afraid of losing her to a man. What could I really say or do to stop her? I felt so sad thinking about it. My stomach was doing flip-flops. What will happen if she starts dating? What if she fell in love with someone and forgot about me? What if a man moved in here with us? I would hate it so much. What if she brought a stranger in and moved him in like dad did with Lindy?

Just then, I felt like I was going to throw up. I jumped up and ran to the bathroom. I heard mom calling my name as I reached the toilet. I leaned over and dry heaved a few times. Mom came in and stood at the door.

"Are you okay?" she asked.

"Yes, I just want to go to my room," I replied as I stood up and regained my composure.

She put her hand on my shoulder as I walked by her. "Hunny, please...," she said as I kept walking.

I went to my room and threw myself on the bed as tears gushed out and smeared my cheeks. It didn't take mom too long to come in and sit on my bed beside me.

I sat up, still crying. Mom started rubbing my back. I tried to talk, but I couldn't catch my breath long enough to say anything. Mom pulled me close to her and held me tight. It felt really good to just let it all out. It was comforting to be in mom's arms and it made me cry even harder.

All the emotions I had built up inside me about the divorce seemed to come out all at once.

I cuddled up to her and tried to calm myself. Mom stroked my hair and held me until I calmed down enough to talk. I sat up and looked at her. She looked so sad. I sat there a minute while mom rubbed my back.

"Mom, I don't want you to date anybody. I want it to be you and me," I said once I finally calmed down enough to talk.

"Sam, I don't want to be alone the rest of my life. I want someone to share my life with," she said as she rubbed my back.

I felt a stab at my heart as she spoke these words. It really hurt my feelings that I couldn't be the person she wanted to share her life with.

"What's wrong with me? I'm not good enough?" I said in a small voice.

Mom stopped rubbing my back and threw her arms up in the air in frustration. She spoke sternly, "Samantha, you are my life! I love you with all of my heart, but someday you will have your own family and where will I be then? I don't want to live my years alone when you are grown up and have your own life."

"Then I won't leave you. I will never leave you, mom, I promise," I said, pleading with her.

With that being said, I started to cry again, pleading ever so much with her to be happy with just the two of us. Anything so she doesn't go out and find a new relationship. I wanted to be the person that she loves the most.

"Hunny, you just don't get it. It's lonely being in my shoes," she said as she pulled me closer to her.

I interrupted her, hoping to convince her otherwise about dating. "But you said dad was the only man for you."

"Yes, I did, but that was a while ago. See, when your father first left, I felt so lonely and hurt. I felt like nobody would ever love me again. I had to go out and find a job to support us and get used to a new life. I was tired, worried and completely stressed out. The man I loved and thought I would spend the rest of my life with suddenly had no love to give back. I was ready to give up on life. Now, I feel better about myself, and I finally want to go out and live life again. I am ready to venture into the dating world and see what comes of it. It's not like I am going to run out and grab any man and bring him home with me. It won't be like that," she concluded.

I was very surprised she opened up to me like this. I have never heard her speak so openly about her feelings. I really cried then. What if she left me like dad did? Then I would have no place to go. Nobody would take care of me. I thought of what it would be like to live on the streets with no food or shelter. Then, I cried harder than ever.

I spoke between the sobs, "I don't want you to find anybody. Please, mom, I love you. I want you to always be there for me. I don't want you to be like dad. Please don't leave me, mom!"

"Oh, baby, I would never leave you. You will always be by my side. I promise I won't ever love you any less, no matter what the circumstance. You will always come first in my life, sweetheart," mom said as she held me tight.

I felt so much better when she said that. I still didn't like the idea of her trying to find a new companion, but at least she promised she wouldn't throw me aside like dad did. She sure knows what to say when I am feeling down. That is the best part of having her as a mom. A little part of me still thought, what if....I was relieved, but scared at the same time.

Before long we were in the kitchen fixing an evening snack. Just the two of us. I embraced the moment, thinking someday it might not be this way. We took our snacks with us and returned to our monopoly game. We were having a good time together until the phone rang.

Mom answered it and her voice instantly changed once she found out who it was. She told them to hold on a minute and looked at me apologetically.

"We'll finish the game later, Okay?" mom said as she stood up. I nodded; she blew me a kiss and went to her room.

Mom was still in her room an hour later. I was bored and growing tired of waiting. I flipped through the television channels, looking for something to watch. I finally got up and went to my room. I figured she would call me when she was ready.

The next thing I knew, it was time for bed. I went downstairs and put the game away, knowing it was over. I felt angry that she would just blow me off that easily. She was probably talking to Martha. I muttered, "Stupid Martha!" under my breath as I walked back to my room.

I put on my pajamas and waited for mom to come in and tell me goodnight. I lay there for a long time, just waiting and waiting for her to come in.

Finally, I grew too tired and just shut off the light and lay in the dark. I felt hurt that she didn't at least pop her head in and say good night. I felt like I didn't even matter to her.

My thoughts went to what mom said earlier. I whispered, "I will always come first...yeah, right...that's why you run into your room and forget about me."

The thought of losing my mom to someone else made my stomach turn over. What if she really did find someone? What if they didn't like me? There goes the idea of mom and dad getting back together someday. I really hoped for Lindy to leave dad so he would come back home. I guess that won't happen if mom isn't even waiting for him.

As I drifted off to sleep that night, I dreamt of all kinds of men roaming our house, going from room to room. They were everywhere. They never spoke, just walked from one room to another. Each one who looked in my room would glare at me like I wasn't supposed to be there. They wanted me gone.

Chapter Four

Mom is Dating

After mom told me she wanted to start dating, she instantly started acting funny. One time, I caught mom staring off into space with a stupid smile on her face. Another time, she wasn't even home when I got home from school. I was afraid something happened to her. She was always home when I got off the bus.

She doesn't even act like my mom anymore. She acts more like a giddy teen. When I ask her what is going on, she just hugs me and sighs.

She and Martha used to sit at the table and talk. Now, they are going into her room more and more. It irritates me when they go into her room and close the door. It's like they have a secret they are hiding from me. I can hear them giggling sometimes and it just makes it worse. I feel so left out. I know they are hiding something and guess who they are hiding it from... Yep, that would be me. I despise Martha more now than ever before. When she is around, I feel like an outsider.

I have been trying to get to the bottom of all the whispering, but haven't been very successful. I even put my ear to mom's bedroom door a few times to see if I could hear them. They whisper so quietly I can't make out a single word.

Today, Martha came over again. She seems to be coming over almost every day now. I am so sick of her. I just roam the house wondering what they are whispering about, and it drives me crazy.

I usually just go to my room, sit on my bed and wonder how I can find out what is going on. I find myself racking my brain and trying to figure out why mom is acting so strange. I thought and thought, and boom! It hit me like a brick! She started acting weird ever since she mentioned dating! I thought about her staring off into space with a big smile; that's it! She has a boyfriend!

My heart skipped a beat, then sank to my feet. I felt shaky all over. Oh no! That cannot be happening. I tried not to think about it but just couldn't help it. A tear started down my cheek as I begged God not to let this happen. Don't let it be, Dear God, oh please…don't let it be. I sat there a long time trying to gather myself together. I stayed in my room, trying to keep myself busy until Martha left.

Before long, I heard mom's bedroom door open, and suddenly, they were talking in a normal tone. I could hear everything they were saying. It was all small talk. I heard Martha say she had to get going, and I let out a sigh of relief. I was so glad she was finally leaving.

I heard the door close, and mom was fiddling in the kitchen, so I decided to go talk to her. I leaned on the counter as she started cooking supper.

"Hey, how are you?" she asked as she glanced over at me and smiled.

"Okay," I replied.

"And how was school today?" She asked as she put a pot on the stovetop.

"Fine," I said as I tried to act casual.

I started chewing my nails as the small talk continued. I hoped she would open up and tell me what was going on, but she didn't.

We ate supper and started cleaning up. I knew I would have to ask her what was up, but I was scared and too nervous to ask. I didn't want to hear she had a boyfriend. That would be the worst.

I began to wash dishes while mom put the food away. I thought, now or never, so I began, "Mom, why do you and Martha go in your bedroom to visit now?"

She stopped what she was doing and looked at me. I kept washing dishes to keep from showing how nervous I was. She picked up a bowl of food and put it in the fridge.

"Maybe we need to sit down and discuss some things when we are finished with the kitchen," she said matter-of-factly.

As I finished the dishes and dried my hands, She walked over to the table and sat down. She motioned for me to sit in the chair next to her.

"Come sit."

I couldn't help but roll my eyes as I walked over. These chats always seem to have a way of affecting my life in a bad way.

Mom grabbed my hand and fiddled with it as she began, "Hunny, remember when I told you I was ready to date?"

I think she was pretty nervous, but I probably held first place in nervousness. Especially since she had such a serious look on her face, which made me even more afraid of what she was about to say. She paused for a long time. The tension in the room was growing thicker.

She finally said, "I am seeing someone."

I was speechless. I sat there trying to digest what she just said. I knew it. I was right. My mom had a boyfriend. What would happen to me? Will she be just like dad and throw my feelings away? Will it be someone who hates me? I looked down at the table and shook my head. This can't really be happening.

I stood up, instantly angry. I hollered, "So stupid Martha finally won. She finally talked you into it, didn't she? She talked you into dating that stupid guy, didn't she? Is it him? Is it the one she bugs you about? I hate her!"

I started to run to my room, but mom grabbed me. I tried to squirm away, but it was no use.

"Samantha Louise, you are going to sit your butt down and listen to me!" she said as she walked me over to the table. I could tell she was not fooling around, so I stopped struggling and defiantly plopped in the chair. I crossed my arms in anger. I wanted to scream at her but knew I better not push it.

Mom sat down and gave me the angriest look. She started in her lecture tone. "You do not and never will run my life! You better get that straight right now!" she spoke between clenched teeth.

I felt a lump in my throat as I held back the tears. Mom let out a sigh.

She lowered her tone and continued, "Yes, I have been seeing the guy Martha talked about. He's a great guy and I will not stand for you to mess things up. I will continue to see him whether you like it or not. You know I love you, and seeing him will not make me love you any less."

I banged my hands on the table and yelled, "But you didn't even tell me! You've been running in your room with Martha and being sneaky about it!"

Mom grabbed my hands and spoke with a tone I never heard

before. "You listen here, little girl, you will not be banging on the table and talking to me like that again. I am your mother, and I will not stand for that. I have every right in the world to have my own privacy. I don't have to tell you every detail in my life. If I want to go to my room and talk privately, I will. I am the adult here, not you."

With that being said, I burst into tears. Mom has never talked to me like that, and I had no idea how to handle it. She sat there and just looked at me. She didn't even hug me or try to comfort me or anything. That made me feel even worse. I cried even harder. I covered my face with my hands and poured out tears.

Mom got up and left the table. I thought she didn't even care. How could she leave me there crying like that? The next thing I know she comes back in the room and hands me some Kleenex. She sat down.

She waited for me to stop sobbing and began, "Samantha, you should know why I didn't tell you what was going on. You were so upset about me even mentioning dating that I didn't think you were ready for the news. I didn't think it would be wise to tell you just yet. I was afraid of how you would react, and Look ... this is exactly why. Hunny, you are going to have to grow up a little bit. You need to realize that you can't control other people. All you can do is control your own self and learn to adjust to those around you. I am happy when I am with you, and I am happy when I am with Carl."

So that's his name, Carl. I didn't know what to say. I felt confused and angry. Mom has never treated me this way before. She is usually right there to comfort me in her arms. I had no idea how to act or what to do.

I forced myself to whisper I'm sorry and asked to be excused. Mom nodded, and I went to my room. I lay on my bed for a long time, just staring blankly at the stars on my ceiling. They glowed in the dark at one time but didn't anymore. Kind of like… you glow at times, but after a while, the light dims. Gloomy.

That's how I felt. More changes are coming, and I am so tired of changes in my life. I didn't want things to change anymore. I was so miserable. I tried to see things mom's way, but I knew I would never do this to my kids when I grow up. Who knows, She might even be right. I just couldn't see her point, but then again, what do I know about love? All I know is I hate it! It already took dad away from me, and now it's taking mom away from me. I wondered when she would start taking time away from me to go see him. It just isn't fair.

That night mom came into my room to say good night. I kept my eyes on the ceiling and pretended she wasn't there. I didn't want to respond to her. She hesitated, told me she loved me and closed the door.

The next morning, I got up and started getting ready for school. I felt like I was hit by a Mack truck. It was like I had a horrible weight on me that I couldn't shake. I moved slowly and just could not pick up my pace. I heard the sound of the bus and ran to catch it. Shoot! I missed it! I saw the bus pulling away as I opened the door. Great. Mom wouldn't be home until 8:30, and I didn't want to be tardy again. My eyes were all puffy, and I looked terrible. I definitely didn't want to be late and have all eyes on me today.

I had no choice but to call Martha. Just the person I wanted to see. She was so sneaky, and all she did was try to ruin my life. She had it in for me. I found her phone number hanging on the fridge and dialed it. She sounded like she was still sleeping.

"Martha, it's me, Samantha. I missed the bus," I said, wishing I didn't have to talk to her at all.

"Okay, I'll be there in five minutes," she said through a yawn.

When I got in her car, I couldn't look at her. I made it very obvious I was mad at her.

She looked over at me and asked, "Why the cold shoulder?"

I just shrugged my shoulders and stared at my feet. I couldn't wait to get to school and get away from her. The drive seemed to take forever.

My whole day at school was a blur. I couldn't concentrate on any of the lessons, no matter how hard I tried. I took a science test and didn't do well at all. I couldn't even comprehend the questions, so I just circled any answer. Good thing it was multiple choice.

My best friend, Tricia kept asking me what was wrong but I just kept telling her nothing. I didn't want to talk about it.

Soon, it was time to go home. I didn't really want to face mom. I stepped off the bus and went into the house, dreading every second of it. I let out a sigh of relief when she was nowhere to be seen. I headed straight for the bedroom and stayed in there until mom called me for supper time. I couldn't avoid her any longer. Here goes...

I was confronted about being snotty to Martha and about my attitude toward her. I was nagged at the whole time we sat at the table. Oh, joy! As soon as supper was cleaned up, I went back to my room.

The rest of the week I couldn't sleep much. It really bothered me to hear Martha and mom whispering and giggling in her room like school kids all the time. Especially now that I know what they're talking about.

I would come home from school and go straight to my room. I stayed there most of the time, trying to avoid mom as much as possible. I would cry often, wondering what happened to us. I guess mom probably cried a lot, too, because her eyes were swollen and red most of the time.

I spent most of my time on the phone with Tricia as I lay across my bed. I hardly spoke to mom. I wasn't in any mood to listen to her lectures anymore. Besides, I was still mad at her.

Tricia and I talked about things that happened in school and about boys. I didn't tell her about mom and me. I was still too hurt and angry to talk about it.

After a few days, mom wouldn't even come in to tell me good night. I could hear her footsteps coming down the hall and pausing at my door. I would wait for her to open it, but she would continue walking down the hall to her room. This made me even angrier at her. Even If I didn't respond to her, she could at least tell me goodnight. It would make me feel like she still cared about me. I felt so lonely without her.

I couldn't wait to go to dad's just to get away from all the stress. I even had my bags packed a day early. The last two weeks seemed so long to me. One more day and I will be able to get away. I couldn't stop thinking about asking dad if I could live with him. I knew his answer would be no since I didn't even have a room there, but I really wanted to ask him anyway. Just knowing he would probably say no made me not able to sleep. I tossed and turned all night. I was so anxious to get out of here, I just couldn't stand it! I wanted to go to dad's now and never come back here again.

Chapter Five

Off to Dad's at Last

Finally, it was Friday, and I couldn't wait to leave for the weekend. School seemed to drag on forever. I kept watching the clock through the whole day, just wishing it would get over. As soon as I returned home, I ran to my bedroom to get my stuff. I packed up my last-minute things and turned toward the door.

"Ready and waiting to go!" I murmured under my breath. As I picked up my suitcase and headed for the door, I suddenly froze.

Mom was standing in my doorway. I just stood there, looking at her. She was all dressed up. Boy, did she look pretty! I wasn't about to compliment her. I could just about guess where she was going. Yep, out with that Carl guy.

I couldn't wait to leave. Then, reality hit me. She probably couldn't wait for me to leave, either. That only made me angrier. I wanted to take my stuff and walk right by her, but she stood there, taking up all the space. Since I knew I couldn't get by her, I just put my suitcase down and sat on the edge of my bed. I made sure to face away from her so I didn't have to see her.

"Samantha," she said in a broken voice. "I don't want you to leave mad."

I just nodded my head. I didn't have anything to say.

"Listen," she said as she clasped her hands together. "You have been so angry and irritable. You need to accept things you cannot change. You aren't just making it miserable for me, but you are making life miserable for you, too." Mom paused and let out a sigh.

I think she knew it wasn't going to work. "I guess I just want you to know I love you," she said in a small voice.

I just sat there, not knowing what to say. My heart started to melt from her words. I wanted to run into her arms and cry, but I held my ground and sat there, acting like it didn't faze me. Mom stood there a minute (which seemed like hours) and slowly walked away. I kind of felt bad for her, but she kind of deserved it. She made me feel bad, too.

Just as I put my bags in the living room, dad pulled up and beeped the horn. It was time to go. I looked around for mom, but she wasn't anywhere to be found. I noticed her bedroom door was closed and figured she must be in her room. I slowly walked my things to the door. I put my shoes on, watching her door the whole time. I secretly hoped she would come out and say goodbye, but why would she when I wouldn't even speak to her? It felt so lonely leaving the house without anyone to say goodbye to. I wondered if that was how mom feels when she leaves for work every night.

I felt lousy as I carried my bags across the yard. I guess I might be treating her a little unfair. I had my chance to make it up to her, and I blew it. Why am I being so mean? I ruined the moment by being stubborn. How stupid can I be? Now I really felt miserable. I really know how to screw things up sometimes.

I looked up and saw dad walking toward me. "Hey," he said as he bent over to kiss my cheek. I gave him a big fake smile and a very small "hi". I tried really hard to sound cheerful.

"It's pretty cold out here," he said as he grabbed my bags from me. He loaded my stuff in the back of the truck while I jumped in.

As we backed out of the driveway, I watched the house intensely, just hoping for mom to come out and at least wave to me. Just as dad put the truck in drive, I heard, "Samantha! Samantha!" It was mom! I was so happy and relieved! She waved her arms in the air, hollering my name over and over.

"Wait, Dad! It's Mom!" I said, full of excitement.

He stopped and pulled over to the edge of the road. I jumped out of the truck and went running to her. She swept me up in her arms and gave me the greatest hug I ever had. I didn't realize how much I missed her hugs until then. Just thinking about it made me tear up. She gave me a big kiss on the cheek and ruffled my hair. I could see by her puffy red eyes that she had been crying in her room.

Fresh tears lingered on her cheeks as she said, "I love you, Samantha."

"I Love you too," I said as I hugged her again. Tears were flowing freely on both of us by then.

Mom looked me in the eyes and gave me that beautiful smile of hers. She said, "You have a good time at your dad's."

"I will," I replied. "You look so pretty," I said, smiling back at her. It was such a silly thing to say at the moment, but I just had to tell her how pretty she was.

"Thanks, Sam," she said, somewhat surprised.

She hugged me and kissed me one more time, and we parted ways. I jumped back in the truck, feeling a hundred times better. I watched mom out the window as we pulled away. She blew me a kiss, and I pretended to catch it.

Dad kept glancing over at me, giving me a strange look as he drove. I tried to hide my face so he wouldn't see that I had been crying, but I think he already knew it. We drove down the road for a few minutes, and suddenly dad broke the silence.

"Sooo, you want to share what that was all about?" he asked nonchalantly.

I looked at him, teary eyes and all. I smiled and said, "No."

I was happy for the first time in two long weeks, and explaining all that happened would ruin it. Telling dad about it would only make me sad again. I wanted to keep the good feeling I had for as long as I could.

That evening was a blast! Me, dad and Lindy played charades most of the night. We laughed so much my stomach hurt! Everybody was just being plain silly. It was nice to laugh and be light-hearted for a change.

Later in the evening, we all sat together on the couch and watched a movie. I fell asleep halfway through it.

I woke up in the middle of the night, sat up and looked around. Then I remembered I was at dad's house. Dad and Lindy must have gone to bed. I laid back down and slept the rest of the night.

When morning came, dad sat next to me on the couch. I woke up from it but didn't move. I could hear Lindy in the kitchen making breakfast. I listened to the sizzling of bacon in between the clanging pans and the fridge opening and closing.

Dad nudged me, "Hey, you awake?" I turned toward him and barely opened my eyes.

"I am now," I said with a half smile. It felt good to have him waking me up. I really miss him being around all the time.

"So, are you going to tell me what was up with you and your mom?" he asked light-heartedly.

I turned around and buried my head in the pillow. "Oh, Dad, I just woke up," I groaned.

"Lindy will be going grocery shopping later on today. You want to talk then?" he asked.

I moaned, keeping my head in the pillow. I replied, mumbling, "No, Dad."

He nudged me again, "Oh, come on, Samantha, you can talk to me. I need to know what is going on in that little brain of yours." He ruffled the back of my head as he spoke.

"Oh, okay…" I said as I snuggled into the couch a little more and wished I could disappear...

"Promise?" he asked. I didn't answer. He peered over and put his face real close to me. I turned my head toward him and opened my eyes. I could tell he was up to something. He was right in front of my face, making silly faces at me. It made me smile, and we both giggled a bit.

"Promise?" he repeated as he held out his pinky.

"Okay, I promise," I said to him as I giggled. I just couldn't resist him. We locked pinkies for our pinky promise, and it was done. Now I have to talk to him. He was just too smooth. It wasn't exactly how I wanted to spend time with him, though.

Dad stood up and said, "Okay, it is time to rise and shine. Breakfast will be ready soon. I am going to go help Lindy finish up."

At that, he walked into the kitchen. I sat up and stretched with my arms way above my head and yawned. It was nice to see Dad first thing in the morning. I felt mixed feelings because I felt good about being with him, but I felt anxious about talking with him about mom and me. I knew he wasn't going to let me off the hook with a pinky promise involved. I will have to tell him what happened between us. The last thing I wanted to do was talk to him about mom dating someone. The thought made me groan as I stood up and went into the bathroom to freshen up.

Before I knew it, breakfast was ready. We all sat down at the table and ate. I helped Lindy clean up. I thought she might like my help since she made such a delicious breakfast. She put some effort into it, and I wanted to show my appreciation. She was very thankful for my help.

I found my bags and rummaged through them for some clothes to wear. I took a shower, brushed my teeth and got ready for the day.

When Lindy started getting ready to leave, I went into the living room and sat down. It stressed me out to think of what is coming next. I really didn't want to talk to dad about this.

Lindy left, and dad came into the living room to sit by me. As soon as he looked at me, I burst into tears. He wrapped his arms around me and comforted me. Once I settled down, I looked at him and smiled. He really was a great father.

"Pumpkin, you are really making me wonder what is going on," he said in a concerned voice.

I pulled away from him, trying to figure out where to even start. I had no idea how he would take knowing that mom was dating. Would he get mad or sad? I wasn't sure how he would feel about it.

"Mom, she…" I stumbled as I searched for the right words. I continued to ramble, "She is…well,…seeing this…guy…" I paused and held my breath.

He looked at me, waiting for more. He finally put his palm up and said, "And?"

Words came easier this time. He acted like it was no big deal.

"She's seeing him… you know, dating him," I said in almost a whisper. It seemed like a forbidden thing to me.

Dad shrugged his shoulders and asked, "Is that bad?"

I looked up at him. He looked lost. He definitely didn't understand. He waited for me to reply. He then asked, "Don't you like him?"

I told him I have never met him, but Martha has been pushing mom to go out with him forever.

Dad was acting like he was so confused. He asked, "If you don't even know him, then what is the problem?"

I couldn't believe he didn't even care if she dated someone else! I really thought it would hurt his feelings. I was at a total loss for words. I didn't want her time taken away from me, but I didn't know how to convey that to dad. He had Lindy, so I guess he probably wouldn't understand how I felt.

I felt my eyes begin to burn as I looked at dad. I finally blurted out, "I just don't want her to see anybody."

I put my hands up in the air and dropped them down in defeat. I started to cry again in frustration.

Dad adjusted on the couch and said, "Listen, Sam, your mom deserves to go out and have fun. She can't just work and cater to everyone else's needs all her life."

"I know, Dad, but she can have fun with other people," I interrupted. He stopped and looked at me, saying, "Like who?"

I said, "Family, friends."

I looked up at him and added, "Me," in a very small voice.

Dad nodded as a spark appeared in his eyes. I think he suddenly understood. He gave me a little smile and said, "Oh, I see… you are a little jealous, are you?"

I quickly responded, "Not! I just think it takes away from our time together, that's all."

Dad relaxed a bit and said, "Pumpkin, she isn't going to love you any less just because she is seeing someone." "But I need her!" I blurted out.

"I know; she needs you too. She can date and still be your mom at the same time. It sounds like you need to back off a bit and give her some space. She needs to be able to make her own decisions in her life. She can't let everybody else determine how her life goes, Especially her twelve-year-old daughter," he said as he pointed at me.

Wow, that didn't go well. Now, dad is siding with mom. Of course he is, he is living with Lindy. Why would it bother him? It hurt my feelings that nobody was thinking of me. It made me realize that adults didn't think of how kids feel at all.

Dad must have seen the frustration in my face. He said, "Listen, your mom is an adult and has the right to make her own decisions. You need to chill out and let her be. Don't you be giving her a hard time about it, either. Changes come in life, and you have to learn to accept them and live with them. If you don't, you will end up being an angry little girl that nobody wants to be around."

I sat there quietly, surprised at what dad was saying. I couldn't believe what I was hearing! This is something that changes my whole life, and he acted like it was nothing.

"You grouch!" he said in a deep voice as he reached over and tickled me.

I am super ticklish, and he knew it. He kept tickling me and I laughed so hard I had a stomach ache! It made me realize how good it felt to laugh like that. He definitely knew how to lighten my mood.

We sat there for a bit, just gazing out the window. Dad finally spoke, "Just give your mother some slack and try to learn to deal with it, sweety. She deserves to be happy. Besides, if she is happy, it should make you happy."

"I know," I sighed, "but it makes me feel horrible."

"I am not trying to be hard on you, I know it makes you feel bad and all, but you'll get used to it. I know you have gone through lots of changes in the past year. I can only hope you can accept it all and move forward. Please, just do not let it make you an angry, irritable soul. I believe you are way too smart to let that happen."

"But Dad, I am so mad at her!" I exclaimed with my hands in fists.

"I'm warning you right now, little girl, you better be respectful to your mom, or you will have to answer to me," he said with sternness.

I swallowed hard as a lump formed in my throat. Dad's voice changed, and I knew he was quite serious. I didn't expect this kind of reaction from him.

I nodded and let out a small, "Okay."

He stopped, shook off the whole thing and hugged me. It was over just like that.

"I have to go into the garage and find out what is wrong with Lindy's car. Are you going to be okay in the house alone?" Dad asked as he stood up. I nodded.

"If you need anything, you know where to find me." He said as he pointed toward the back door. I smiled at him.

He leaned over and kissed my forehead. I waited for him to leave, but he just stood there. I looked up at him and quickly turned away. His gaze made me feel uneasy. He took my chin in his hand and turned my face toward him. No chance of avoiding those eyes now.

"Never forget how much I love you," he said, "And your mother loves you just as much."

He stood there a little longer, then left for the garage. I sat there a minute digesting what just happened. I guess nobody will understand. I decided that I would just pretend it wasn't happening and act like everything was normal. I didn't know how to get used to it, as dad had put it. If I pretended it wasn't happening it would be better.

Sunday came fast. Dad and Lindy both took me home. She was a lot nicer to me ever since Dad had a talk with us. I was nicer to her, too, because I didn't want to answer Dad for being mean.

Mom came out on the front porch when we pulled in. I was so happy to see her out on the porch waiting for me. Maybe she really won't forget about me after all. Is it just my imagination running wild? I shook off my thoughts and gave dad a hug and kiss goodbye. I said bye to Lindy and got out of the truck.

Dad got out of the truck, too, and grabbed my suitcase. He started carrying it to the house. I gave mom a great big bear hug, and we all went inside, where it was warm.

Dad put my suitcase down and stood there like he had something to say. I went over and gave him a hug goodbye but he still didn't move. It made me nervous because he normally brought my stuff in and left.

Mom noticed he was fidgeting and took a few steps toward him. "Is everything okay?" she asked with concern.

"Yeah," he replied, "I just wanted to talk to you for a second." "Sure," she said and motioned him to sit at the table.

I took my suitcase and went to my room. I sure didn't want to stick around and find out what was going on. Would he tell mom about our talk? I hoped not. I could hear their voices but couldn't make out anything they were saying. My heart skipped a beat as I thought about what he was telling her. I hoped Dad wasn't mad at mom or anything. It would be my fault if he was.

Chapter Six

Tricia's Little Party

After thinking about it, the conversation I had with Dad did help a little. I still didn't quite understand everything, but I felt a little better anyway. I decided to be nicer to mom instead of showing her how mad I was at her. Even if I didn't want her to see this guy, being cordial would at least make things easier at home.

I kept reminding myself to pretend everything is okay. Mom and I were getting along just fine as long as we didn't talk about Carl. The second she mentioned his name, I would clam up. She noticed and eventually stopped trying to talk to me about him.

We spent lots of time together, shopping, going out to eat or just hanging out at the house. We even went to the movies.

Mom bought me two outfits and some underwear that I desperately needed. I wondered where she even got the money to do all of this fun stuff with her, but I never asked her. I was just happy to be able to spend my time with her. We were having so much fun!

On Friday, my friend Tricia asked if I could spend the night with her. She was having a slumber party with a few friends. We were going to be camping in a tent in Tricia's backyard. Carrie was coming over, too. She is Tricia's cousin. She is pretty cool.

I asked mom if I could go when I got home from school. She called Tricia's mom and talked to her about it. When she hung up the phone, I anxiously waited for an answer. She said it was okay. I hugged her, thanked her and ran off to my room to pack.

I packed up my things and waited for mom to finish dusting. The next thing you know, mom was in the kitchen making grilled cheese. I rolled my eyes behind her back. She was always worried about me not eating when I went to someone's house. It's crazy since it was only about 3:30. It's not like they are going to skip supper. I just took the sandwich and ate it to keep the peace. There's no use in arguing with mom. You'll never win. The quicker I eat it, the sooner we will be on our way.

Mom took me to Tricia's house. We finally made it there. I jumped out of the car and opened the back door to get my stuff out. Mom jumped out and circled the car to tell me goodbye. She hugged and kissed me and told me to have a good time. I told her I loved her, and off I skipped down the sidewalk to the front door.

Tricia and Carrie stood in the open doorway, waiting for me to get up to the porch. I could tell they were all wound up. They each grabbed a bag from my hand and ran toward Tricia's room. I had to pick up the pace just to keep up with them. They were giggling like crazy, and I knew they were up to something.

Before Tricia even closed the door, Carrie knelt down and reached under the bed. "All clear?" Carrie asked.

Tricia shut the door, locked it and replied, "Yep."

The next thing you know, Carrie pulled out these sexy books and laid them all out on the bed. "This is our reading material for the tent," Carrie said with enthusiasm. She then started to giggle. Tricia joined in and both of them giggled spastically. I just stood there in shock, looking at the covers. I was so surprised to see them. This is not at all what I expected. Every one of the women were in bikinis that looked like they were too small for them. They were all sitting on motorcycles and posing beside cars.

"Where did you get these?" I asked.

Tricia sat on the bed next to the magazines. She said, "Carrie brought them."

Carrie spoke up, "My dad's room. He won't miss them for one night." She gathered them up and stuck them back under the bed. I was floored but also very curious about what we would find inside the magazines. I guess we will find out later tonight.

We messed around in Tricia's room for a while, talking girl talk and showing each other the makeup we brought. A few other girls showed up as we chatted.

Around five o'clock, Tricia's mom called us downstairs. She hollered, "Girls, pizza's here!"

I wasn't even hungry, but pizza is pizza. Gotta have it anyway. I didn't breathe a word about the grilled cheese I had earlier. I wouldn't want anyone to think I was a pig. Needless to say, I looked like a light eater with only one piece of pizza and a small breadstick. (along with an overstuffed belly) If only they knew…

After supper, we went outside to set up our tent. Tricia's dad helped us so it went up pretty fast. We finished up and went inside to get our sleeping bags and clothes. Carrie packed the magazines in her bag, and off we went to spend the evening in the tent.

We told secrets at first, gossiping about different people we knew. Then we played truth or dare. I chose truth every time because I am not all that brave. I guess you could call me a chicken.

Before you knew it, we were talking about boys. They were all talking about who they had a crush on. I sat there quietly, hoping they wouldn't notice my silence. I didn't want anyone to ask me who I liked.

Tricia was rambling, "Oh, you gotta meet Toby. He's so cute! Isn't he Sam?"

I replied, "Yeah, he is."

Tricia continued, "Carrie, you just gotta meet him! And he likes me too!"

"Really?" I asked. That was news to me.

"Yeah, he wrote me a letter and told me so. I was so excited!" she exclaimed.

"When did this happen?" I asked, hurt by her not telling me earlier.

"Today," she replied. Tricia pulled a note out of her pocket and proudly handed it over to me. Carrie hunkered over my shoulder as we both read it. I handed it back with a big smile. Tricia folded it back up carefully and stuck it in her pocket.

Tricia turned to Carrie and asked, "What about you? Do you have a boyfriend?"

"Kind of," she hesitated, "This boy, Cory." She looked all dreamy-eyed as she sighed. "He's so cute!" she exclaimed as her eyes lit up. She continued, "He doesn't know I like him, though. I would die if he found out!"

"Why?" Tricia asked.

"Well, we flirt back and forth a lot. We even danced together at the last school dance, but the rumor is that he likes this other girl in our school," she said as she trailed off in deep thought.

Tricia chimed in and broke her thoughts, "Come on, you have to at least let him know you like him."

"What if he doesn't like me back?" she asked as her eyes narrowed.

"But what if he does?" Tricia inquired, "You worry too much. What if he finds another girlfriend just because you didn't let him know you liked him?"

Tricia continued to pick at her about telling Cory she liked him. Carrie started to look uneasy about the whole situation after a while. Finally, I told Tricia she should probably leave it alone for a bit. She can be so annoying sometimes. She just doesn't know when to stop.

Carrie suddenly looked at me quizzingly, and out came the big question. She asked, "What about you? Do you have a boyfriend?"

Oh no! Here I am, trying to stick up for her, and she just turns it all around toward me. Great! I really didn't want to talk about it. I had a boy in mind but would not dare say a word. Tricia had a big mouth and would tell him.

"I… uh… really don't like anyone," I said as I tried to hide my true thoughts.

Tricia put in her two cents, which didn't help any. "I know you too well, Sam. That look in your eyes tells it all. Who is it?"

"I…well..uh…" I just didn't want to tell them.

Then, all the girls cued in and started heckling me. They were all talking at the same time, saying Who is it? Who is it? Come on, Samantha, say who it is! Tell us!

I looked around at the girls, wondering if I should tell them. Carrie was the only safe bet because she didn't go to our school. She would be the only one who wouldn't let out my secret crush. Tricia was in the same class as Jake and I. Would she tell him? It would be my worst nightmare come true if he were to find out that I liked him.

Tricia had a huge smile on her face as she spoke, "Do you think we are going to let you get away with not telling us? Come out with it!"

I knew I would have to confess by the way the girls were acting. Besides, Tricia doesn't stop until she gets her way. She is so darn stubborn! Kind of reminds me of my dad. Maybe that's why I like her so much.

Tricia stopped and thought for a minute. She looked at me and asked, "Is it Jake?"

I looked down and didn't speak a word. I felt my face flush and knew it was turning red.

"It is!" she said as she clapped her hands together in victory. "It's Jake, isn't it? I knew it!"

By then, all the girls were hooting and hollering. They all started singing, "You're in love with Ja-a-ake! You're in love with Ja-a-ake!

You're in love with Ja-a-ake!"

I threw my hands down in defeat and said, "Okay, okay, yes, it's Jake." I could tell my face was bright red. I was so embarrassed!

"Look how red her face is!" Tricia said as she pointed at me. They all started giggling and laughing. They thought it was hysterical. They rolled in the tent, laughing and holding their stomachs. The more they laughed, the redder my face got. I even started laughing after a while. Everybody was acting so silly. It was all kind of funny.

It was about midnight when Carrie broke out the magazines. She opened up one, and we all crowded around her.

I was feeling a twinge of guilt and slowly backed up to get away. I didn't want to be a part of this. I noticed Tammy did the same thing I did, so we sat at the back of the tent and talked.

The other girls giggled as she thumbed through the pages. They were laughing at the bikinis the ladies were wearing. As Carrie opened the next magazine, everyone started chatting and goofing around. They all seemed to be losing interest.

Suddenly, the tent started moving. Something was scratching at the side of our tent. We all jumped and let out a scream, and I hugged the closest person to me.

We heard a deep laugh. Tricia chimed in, "Dan! You scared us!" It was Tricia's older brother. It scared the daylights out of us!

"Mom thought you would be ready for a midnight snack," Dan said as he fumbled for the zipper and unzipped the tent.

Carrie closed the magazines and tossed them at me. She whispered," Hurry, hide them!" I didn't know what to do with them. Carrie pointed behind me. I turned around, searching for a hiding place. I finally threw them under my sleeping bag just as Dan jumped in the tent. He handed Tricia the bags of chips and the soda and sat down. He started talking to us. My heart was beating a hundred miles an hour as he looked around the tent. I thought we were going to get busted.

Dan looked around and said, "Man, you girls are messy! There's no place to even sleep!"

Tricia snared at him and pointed toward the door of the tent.

He took note and left. As he zipped the tent door, he said, "Don't let the boogie man get you!"

Tricia yelled, "Shut up, Dan!"

We all relaxed and exhaled. I said, "Whew, that was a close call."

After almost getting caught, we decided to retire the magazines for the night.

I confessed to the girls, "To tell you the truth, I thought they were pretty dumb, anyway."

Everybody agreed, some nodding their heads and others with a quiet "me too." I was relieved to hand the magazines to Carrie and see her pack them up. The mood was ruined by the scare, but it didn't take long to get onto another subject.

We sat up munching on chips and drinking soda half the night. We talked about different things, made promises to each other and told secrets.

When I laid down to sleep, I had a hard time. I couldn't stop feeling guilty about the magazines Carrie brought. They really affected me in a weird kind of way. I wanted to stop thinking about it, but I couldn't. I just felt sick to my stomach from it.

That night, all I did was dream of people in skimpy bikinis. I was walking down this narrow path, and people were walking all around me. They were all like zombies and they all wore bikinis! At the end of the path, I looked up, and there was mom and this man. Mom was wearing a bikini and the man only had on swim trunks. They were kissing! How disgusting! This part jolted me awake. I was up and wide awake then. No way was I going back to sleep and taking a chance to dream that again!

I stayed up most of the night, wondering if boys were worth the trouble. I mean, look at mom and dad. They were so happy, and all of a sudden, they broke up. After twelve years of being married, they just suddenly split up out of the blue. And the fighting was such a short time. I noticed they started fighting a lot about a month before dad moved out. It just doesn't seem possible to ruin a twelve-year marriage in one short month.

I was so glad when the sun began to shine and Tricia woke up. I was driving myself crazy by all the thoughts I conjured up. We chatted for a bit, then decided to wake up the rest of the girls. We plucked a few feathers from Tricia's feather pillow and tickled their noses one by one until they were all awake.

Carrie was the last one to wake up. Tricia tickled her nose with a feather. Carrie smacked her own face a few times, and we all started giggling. When she finally woke up, she jumped Tricia and put her in a headlock. Tricia was laughing hysterically as she tried to wriggle free. We were all cracking up. I pushed Carrie over, and we all started wrestling. It was hilarious.

Tricia's mom came out to get us for breakfast. We were so loud we didn't hear her calling us. As she unzipped the tent, we all jumped and screamed. She scared the daylights out of us!

"What on earth are you guys doing?" she asked as she popped her head into the tent.

"Just messing around," Tricia said as we all laughed at the scare she gave us.

"I have breakfast ready. Why don't you all come in and get something to eat," Tricia's mom said as she turned around and headed for the house.

"Ok," We all said simultaneously, which made us laugh even more.

We ate French toast, sausage and hash browns and wandered into the living room. We loafed around chatting for a bit. Tricia's mom sent us out to clean up the camping equipment early.

She said she had something important come up and she had to leave. She wanted the yard cleaned up before she returned home. As it turned out, Tricia's older sister broke down on the highway and needed her mom to come get her. She had both of her little ones with her.

As we started out the door to clean up the camping mess, Tricia's mom said she would send Dan out to help with the tent in a minute.

"Okay, mom," Tricia replied as we walked out the door.

We all stopped and looked at each other with a worried look on our faces. The next thing you knew, we were all high-tailing it to the tent to hide our dirty underclothes and to make sure the magazines were nowhere to be seen. We stuffed the magazines in Carrie's sleeping bag and rolled them up so they would never be found.

Before long, the camping gear was put away, and we were back in the house watching TV. We hung out in the backyard for a bit but found ourselves back in the house again due to it being a bit cold outside.

Tricia's mom came home, and we played with the little ones for a while. They were so entertaining and so cute!

Tricia's mom finally rounded us up to take us all home. She dropped me off first since I lived the closest. We pulled into the driveway, and I walked up to the front porch. I stopped at the front door, turned and waved to the girls. I went into the house and set my things down to take off my shoes.

Chapter Seven
Meeting Carl

"Mom, I'm home." I hollered.

I thought it was strange she didn't greet me at the door. We came home a little earlier than planned, so I pushed the feeling aside. She just didn't know I was home already. I took my shoes off and grabbed my things. I started toward my room. I wondered where mom was as I walked through the quiet house.

Then it hit me; she must be in her room. She has been spending more and more time there doing God knows what. As I walked toward her room, I noticed her door was shut. The only time she ever shuts her door is when she and Martha are in there whispering back and forth like kids.

I took my things to my room and went to her bedroom door. "Mom?" I called. Much to my surprise, nobody answered.

I walked back toward the kitchen, peeking out the sliding glass door to see if I could catch a glimpse of her in the backyard. I didn't see her, so I opened the door and peeked my head out. She was nowhere in sight.

I raised my voice, this time calling out, "Mom, you there?" I was beginning to wonder if she was even home. Suddenly, the silence felt strange, like something wasn't right.

I went back to the front door and peered out. Her car was in the driveway, but she could have taken off with someone, namely Martha. Mom has a tendency to ride to town with her every now and then. Sometimes, I think Martha takes her on purpose just so she can take my time away from her. I thought again about how much I can't stand that woman.

I finally decided mom had to be gone. She never slept in on Sunday mornings. Even if she did sleep in, she would be awake by now. It was almost eleven o'clock. She would have been up by now, for sure. Besides, she is a light sleeper and would have heard me calling out for her.

I went into my room to unpack my things. The more I thought about mom being gone, the more irritated I became. Did she send me off so she could go do whatever she wanted? Or was something wrong?

I stopped what I was doing as I remembered how she always left a note on the fridge when she went somewhere. I went to go check it out but the fridge was bare. This just wasn't like her to just take off like this. Especially when she knew I was coming home today. Where in the heck was she?

What if Martha drug her off to some bar last night, and something terrible happened to her? What if she did what Dad did and took off with that Carl guy? I ran toward her room, planning to search for a sign. If she left, her clothes would be gone. My heart was beating a hundred miles an hour.

I threw the door open and stopped dead in my tracks. What I saw threw me completely off balance. My feet stopped, but my body continued to launch forward. I fell right to the floor. I lay there hoping and praying this was all a bad dream. I closed my eyes as tears began to overflow and run down my cheeks. I couldn't believe it. I didn't want to look, but I stood up and forced myself to. I had to make sure that I wasn't just seeing things. I wasn't. My eyes were not betraying me as I had hoped.

There was a man sleeping in my mom's bed. I could not believe it. He jolted to sitting position from the noise I made as I fell to the floor. Mom's bathroom door flung open and there stood mom in her robe, with a towel wrapped around her head. She froze with a look of sheer terror in eyes. Tears were streaming down my face so fast I could hardly see. Nobody said a word as I stood there, trying to get a grip on myself.

Finally, I collected my thoughts and turned and ran out of the room. I went straight to my room and locked the door behind me. I threw myself across my bed and cried forever. I just wished I would not have seen what was happening in my mother's room.

It wasn't long before I heard the front door close. I looked out the window and saw a man walking over to Martha's house. He must have parked over there and walked here to stay overnight. How sneaky was that?

They slept in the same room mom and dad slept in for so many years. How can she bring another man into her and dad's room? What a horrible thing to do. My mother has no respect for my dad at all. I despised her at that very moment. I just didn't know her like I thought I did.

I stayed in my room most of the day. Mom tried to come in and talk to me. I didn't want to talk about it. She stood there, just looking at me. I couldn't even look her in the eyes. I just couldn't. How embarrassing it was to see another man in mom's bed with my own eyes. She tried to talk about it, but I pulled the covers over my head and asked her to leave.

Supper was quiet. Not a word was spoken. We both ate mechanically, as if neither one of us were really even there. It felt so awkward to be like this with mom. I think we both wanted to disappear at that moment.

We ate fast, cleaned up quickly and off I went into my room again. I had to keep my mind busy to stop thinking so much, so I cleaned my room and vacuumed my floor. When I was finished, I went through my jewelry box and cleaned my closet. Then I decided to put on nail polish.

Mom came in and told me goodnight, and those were the only words we exchanged that night. I lay in bed for hours, just trying to calm my mind.

Wow, my life would never be the same again. Change is coming. I could feel it. I wondered what was going to happen. Is he going to move in? How could I even look him in the face after such an embarrassing moment? How can I even meet him now? It would be so weird. I just knew it was coming and couldn't stop thinking about the dreaded day I'd have to be introduced to him. How could I act like nothing happened?

My thoughts were racing. I kept thinking of the worst-case scenarios in my head. I tried so hard not to think about it, but I just couldn't stop. I finally fell asleep from exhaustion.

The next thing I knew, I heard someone screaming. The more aware I became, the louder the screaming was. I wondered who was screaming so loud but couldn't wake up enough to figure it out. Then, I realized where it was coming from. It was me! Mom was next to me, holding my arms down. Was I going crazy in my sleep?

Then, I recalled the dream. I was dreaming of mom leaving me by myself. She was moving in with Carl. As I relived the dream, I remember her packing up her stuff from her room. I was screaming and begging her not to leave.

Mom kept telling me to get myself together. She said she was leaving, and nothing could change that. She didn't want to be my mom anymore. She told me in my dream that I was so rotten that nobody would want to be my mom. She stopped at the door, turned toward me, and told me to find someone else to call mom. It was awful!

Thank God it was just a dream! I cried as mom held fast to me. I assumed I was crying in my sleep since my hair was soaked in tears. Although I was still mad at mom, it felt good to be held by her. I didn't want to spoil the moment, so I just held tight to her. I love her so much and she doesn't even realize it. I squeezed her tight, and she squeezed back. I didn't want to ever let go.

Finally, I glanced at the time. I slept for three hours, but It felt like I didn't sleep at all. I snuggled up closer to mom. She ran her fingers through my hair and asked, "Are you okay, honey?" She then kissed the top of my head.

I told her, "Yeah, I think so. I was dreaming," I nodded my head as it lay against her chest. I didn't want to move. I just relished the moment.

She said, "Must have been a pretty bad dream. Can you tell me about it?" I shrugged.

Mom looked down at me and gave me a concerned look as she said, "You can talk to me, sweety."

"I would rather not talk about it right now. I don't even want to think about it," I said as I rubbed my eyes. It felt like I didn't sleep a bit.

Mom pulled me away from her, held my shoulders and looked at me with such an odd look. She leaned over and kissed me on my forehead. She said, "Tell you what, I will go to the kitchen and make us a little midnight snack while you freshen up a bit. How does that sound?"

I nodded my head and smiled through the tears still streaming down my cheeks.

Mom popped up and told me she'd be back as quickly as she could.

I said, "Okay," in a weak voice. I turned my attention to the Kleenex on my vanity. I sat down and dried my face first, then blew my nose. I took a real close look in the mirror and was horrified by my appearance.

I decided to go to the bathroom and wash my face, hoping it would help a little bit. My eyes were so puffy I didn't think anything would help, but it's worth a try.

I washed my face and put some lotion on my bright red cheeks. I returned to my room and sat at my vanity again. Yes, I definitely looked better. I powdered my cheeks and walked over to the bed.

I sat down on the edge of my bed and thought about the dream. I thought about how awful it would be if mom really did leave.

I yawned as I thought about how tired I was. I couldn't lie down because I was afraid I'd fall asleep before mom came back.

Mom returned with Oreos and milk. I tried to force down an Oreo just to make her happy. I felt physically ill from the nightmare and had no desire to eat. Mom ate one, too, as we sat together, making small talk.

Before I knew it, my alarm woke me. It was morning. I reached over and shut off my alarm. I must have fallen asleep in the middle of talking to mom. The last I knew, mom was here, and we were reminiscing about the past while I tried to choke down an Oreo.

I started to roll over and noticed my half-eaten cookie and two empty glasses on my nightstand. I must have klonked out with the cookie in my hand. Mom probably took it from me, placed it there, and tucked me in. I smiled at the thought of mom taking care of me when I needed it most. She really was great.

I got ready for school and slowly wandered around the house. I peeked in mom's room to see if she had gone to work. She was gone, and her bed was neatly made. Looking into her room gave me a flashback from the night before. I shook the awful thought to the back of my mind and walked away, trying not to think of it anymore.

School went okay, but I felt like I was in a daze the whole day. I was so drained of energy. Tricia kept bugging me about the way I was acting. She was driving me crazy! I just wanted to go home and lock myself in my room. I couldn't wait for school to get out. Finally, the last bell rang. I was relieved to go home.

I went into the house, intending to go into my room to hide. Just as I reached the door, mom called me. I stopped, gave out a heavy sigh and went into the living room to see what she wanted.

She was sitting on the loveseat, looking at a photo album. There were albums sprawled all over the place. It looked like such a mess! She never made messes like this.

"Come here, look, it's your fifth birthday," she said as she waved me over.

I walked over and looked at the pictures. I had a party hat on and a party horn in my mouth.

"Just after I snapped this picture you dropped your horn in the cake. You cried so hard because your horn was full of frosting. When we washed it off and thought you were over it, you started crying because your cake was messed up," mom said as she motioned me to sit next to her.

She went through three albums, telling me stories about each picture. It was so boring, but I knew she needed me there. I could tell she was super stressed out by the cracking of her voice every now and then. She seemed to be having a hard time with her emotions. I thought she would start crying any minute, but she didn't. She sure wasn't acting like herself.

Supper time was hard. I had no appetite because I was still upset about the whole situation. I didn't even eat lunch at school. I knew I wouldn't get away not eating with mom around, so I slowly ate. I moved the food around my plate and took small bites every now and then. It took an extra long time to eat because my stomach was still all knotted up. It was so hard to force the food down. Mom seemed to be playing with her food more than eating as well.

She picked up the rolls and tried to pass them to me. "Want a roll?" she asked as she held them out toward me.

"No thanks," I said and shook my head.

"You aren't eating much," she said as she sat the rolls down next to her.

"I ate a lot at lunch today," I lied as I tried hard to sound convincing. I felt bad for lying, but I just couldn't eat anymore. I felt like I would throw up any minute. If she knew I didn't eat lunch she would have made me eat more. I always hated lying to her, but I just had to this time.

Mom stood up and grabbed her plate. She walked it over to the garbage. As she scraped her plate off, she Proclaimed, "I guess my eyes were bigger than my stomach.

I knew she was trying to make excuses for not eating much. I guess we must be a lot more alike than I thought. When we get upset, neither of us can eat much. We are also both very good at ignoring the real problems and pretending they don't exist. (even when it slaps us in the face.)

Mom started clearing the table and putting the food away. I figured this was my chance to scrape my food into the garbage. I didn't want her to see how much was still on my plate. I hardly ate any of it. I took my plate to the sink and started some dishwater. Mom started drying the dishes and putting them away as I washed them. When the last of the dishes were done, I planned to sneak off into my room.

I was almost out of the kitchen when mom called after me, "Samantha."

Dang it! "Yeah?" I replied as I turned toward her.

Mom's expression took me by surprise. She looked so full of anguish. Oh no, here it comes. She's going to talk to me about last night. Mom looked really sad. Her wrinkles were deepened. Not that she had many, but they looked ten times worse than normal. For the first time in my life, she looked old to me. It kind of worried me so I decided I should cooperate with her this time.

Besides that, dad warned me to be respectful to her. I guess that means I have two reasons to be on my best behavior. She sat down in her usual chair. I knew it meant it was time to talk.

I sat down beside her, in dad's old chair. I thought, who cares…he's not here anymore anyway. I never sat in his chair because I always thought he would eventually come home. It may sound silly, but I was secretly saving it for him. I always thought he would be back someday. Now, I know that will never happen. All hope was lost when it came to mom and dad getting back together. He definitely wasn't coming back. I know that now.

Mom looked at me with a very serious expression on her face. I knew it was time to get down to business. I wished I were somewhere else. At Dad's, at Tricia's, anywhere but here, Mom let out a big sigh. I thought, here goes….

"Sam, I am so sorry for what happened yesterday morning. I deeply regret this happened and I hope you can forgive me for not being straight with you. I have not brought him around to meet you because I know how you feel about all of this. I have been doing a lot of thinking and I need to disregard your feelings and live my life, too. I can still care about you, but I also need to move forward in life as well. Carl and I are getting a bit more serious, and I think it is time for a proper introduction for the two of you," she said.

She was really pouring it on. My heart sank as I pleaded with her. I didn't want to meet him after what happened. I stumbled through my words, hoping and praying she would give in.

She held up her hand and interrupted me, "Nothing you say is going to change things. I am going to give you a few days to let this all settle in. Carl will be here Thursday night to have dinner with us."

"I am not meeting him!" I said as I stood up. "I won't! I will stay in my room!"

"You will meet him, and you will be on your best behavior!" mom hollered as she stood up and put her hands on her hips.

"No, I won't!" I yelled as I ran to my room.

I heard her yell, "Get back here, young lady!" just before I slammed the door as hard as I could. What nerve she had to expect me to meet the guy I caught in her room.

Mom stomped down the hallway and tore open my door. She was fiery red and madder than I had ever seen her before.

"You will stop this nonsense right this minute. I have had enough of you and your attitude. I am an adult and will make my own decisions. You will learn to live with whatever I decide to do. I will not sneak around with Carl, for your sake, any longer! You will meet him, and you will be respectful to him. This is your reality check. Learn to deal with it!" She spoke with venom in her voice. It didn't even sound like her!

She stormed out of my room and then came right back in. I never saw her so furious. She came in, placed her hands on her hips and stood there a moment. I hunched over as she glared at me. She took a deep breath and sighed.

"Carl is a very nice man. He wants to meet you, and I have put him off for as long as I can. I am afraid to bring him home to meet you because of your…" She paused, leaned over with her hands on her hips and stressed, "AWFUL ATTITUDE!" Yep, she was really mad.

She continued, "I can't keep you two separated in my life anymore. It is past time for you to straighten up and be decent about this. I care a lot for him, and he is not going to be shoved away just because you seem to have a problem with it. You are meeting him on Thursday, and you will be polite to him. That is the facts!" She turned in a stiff manner and stormed out of my room, slamming the door behind her.

Wow! I never saw her like this before. She was more than mad; she was absolutely furious. I was afraid to do anything after seeing her going off so bad. I stayed as quiet as could be, hoping she wouldn't come back to yell at me again. I know one thing for sure: I will definitely be polite to Carl!

Things were pretty quiet around the house for the next few days. We hardly talked to each other. It was pretty strange the way things were going. I was always the center of attention, and now I didn't know where I stood with mom. I guess I pushed things way too far. I started thinking about how I needed to stop myself from having my little tantrums. Maybe Mom was right. I needed a reality check.

Thursday came and I spent the whole day all stressed out about meeting this ignorant man. I worried all day and he didn't even come. I asked about him when we sat down for supper. Mom said he had some things come up and would try to stop by later. I was relieved when it started getting late, and he wasn't even there yet. I went to bed early that night just to make sure I could avoid him.

My luck ran out on Friday. I came home from school and went to my room to listen to music. I heard the doorbell ring. I turned off my music and waited to see if mom was answering the door. I popped my head out of my bedroom door to listen. I could hear muffled voices coming from the living room. I listened quietly, straining to figure out who it was. I couldn't make out a single word, let alone who was here. I prayed it wasn't Carl. For the first time in my life, I hoped Martha was here.

Deep down in my heart, I knew it was Carl. I wondered if she told him about our little spat and how mad she was at me. I suddenly heard footsteps coming and quickly closed the door. My heart was pounding so hard! I felt like I was going to die if I had to meet this guy today. I was so miserable! I jumped as my door opened.

"Samantha, I have someone I want you to meet," mom said as she closed the door and walked over to me. She quietly warned, "Be on your best behavior."

I wanted to let her know I would be good, but I couldn't even talk. I stood speechless, with my heart beating out of my chest. I finally smiled nervously at her, hoping that would reassure her. She smiled back at me acknowledging she understood. She gave me a quick hug and a pat on the back. We walked out of the room together with her hand still on my back. I was so nervous that I was shaking.

Mom must have felt it because she leaned down and whispered in my ear, "Calm down, hunny. He's really nice, you will like him."

We walked out into the living room together. As Carl spotted us, he stood up. He said, "Aah, This must be Samantha."

He walked toward me with his hand held out. I reached out to shake his hand, and he gently took my hand in his.

He said, "What a beautiful girl you are. It is my pleasure to meet you." He then kissed the top of my hand.

I was taken aback by his charming ways. I smiled at him, not able to speak. No words would match his eloquence, so I thought it would be better not to say a word. Besides, I was pretty embarrassed. I could feel my face turning red. I wondered if he noticed, but he never mentioned it.

We all sat down and talked. Carl asked me a lot of questions about myself. He asked me what grade I was in, how I liked school, what kind of shows I liked, my favorite food, and so much more. He really seemed interested in getting to know me.

He told me he had two boys. One was my age, and the other was ten years old. I guess they live with him. He told me he would bring them over some time so I could meet them.

We all eventually ended up in the kitchen while mom made dinner. I helped her as we chatted back and forth. He really did seem like a nice, genuine guy.

Before long, we were sitting down to eat dinner. It was good, but I didn't eat much. Mom and Carl google eyed each other through the whole supper. I kind of lost my appetite after watching them. It was sort of odd and out of my comfort zone to have this guy sitting at the dinner table with us. It put an empty feeling in my heart. As I looked over at dad's empty chair, I yearned for dad to be there instead of Carl.

We had dinner and went back to the living room to watch some TV. It felt nice; it kind of reminded me of when Dad was around.

Resentment started to creep in as I thought of Dad. Sometimes, I despised him for what he did to mom and me. I mean, he just up and left one day out of the blue. No warning or anything. If it weren't for him, this wouldn't be happening right now. It's confusing to love someone so much and despise them at the same time.

Carl seemed really nice. It surprised me that he wanted to get to know so much about me. He really was a very likable person. Yes, believe it or not, I did kind of like him. I was prepared for the worst, but everything went very well. Mom was lucky to meet such a charming guy. I only hope I can get that lucky someday.

After a while, I decided to go to my room. It was getting late, and I just wanted to listen to some music before I went to bed. I excused myself and said goodbye to Carl. I hung out in my room and listened to music for a bit, then I read my book for a few minutes and went to bed.

I was just dozing off when mom came in. "So what do you think?" she asked as she sat on the edge of my bed.

"I guess he seems okay," I said as I shrugged my shoulders. I didn't want to make it that easy on her. I really liked him, but she didn't need to know. I gave her such a hard time earlier and didn't want to look like a fool for the way I acted.

She pulled the blanket up around me and kissed my forehead. We said our good nights and love yous, and I was off to sleep.

Chapter Eight

Spring Break at Dad's

It was finally time to go to Dad's house. I hadn't seen him for what seemed like forever! I felt sad because he could come to see me whenever he wanted, but he never came between my regular visits. It always hurt my feelings that he wouldn't just pop in and see me here and there. I miss him so much all the time, but I don't think he misses me that much.

Tricia was having a sleepover this weekend. I really wish I could have gone, but I had to go to dad's. I really felt I was missing out again because my parents weren't together. Sometimes, I just feel like a robot, planning each day according to what everybody else wants. It's not like I don't want to go to Dad's. I do want to see him because I miss him. I just wish I wouldn't have to miss hanging out with my friends.

When I got home from school, I started packing my stuff. While I was packing, I heard mom calling out, "Your dad is here, Samantha!"

He came early! I ran around like crazy, throwing my stuff in my suitcase as fast as I could. I heard the door open as I zipped up my suitcase. I looked around my room, hoping I didn't forget anything important.

I heard mom and dad talking as I approached the entry door to set my suitcase down. I went into the kitchen, and there they stood, chatting away like they were the best of friends. I smiled as I secretly thought of how good it felt to see them together in the kitchen. Just like old times.

"Hey girl, how ya doing?" dad asked as he came over and gave me a hug.

"Hi, Dad!" I said as I hugged him back. I really missed him. So much has happened since I last saw him. It just seemed like I hadn't seen him in months. At that instant, all of my resentment over missing Tricia's sleepover dwindled away.

Dad picked up my suitcase and told me he had a surprise for me at the house. I hoped it was a good thing. I needed some good news. I felt such a weight on my shoulders for the past week or so. Meeting Carl confused me so much. He was such a nice guy, but I was leery about him. I didn't want him imposing on me and my mom's life.

As we pulled into dad's driveway, I saw a huge mess in the backyard. There were boards and siding and all kinds of construction materials all over. Then I saw the addition. My eyes lit up as I realized what the mess was all about.

Dad promised he would put on an addition so I could have my own room someday. He finally started it. I jumped out of the truck and ran over to the addition. Dad came up behind me, and I turned to hug him and thank him for getting things started. I was so excited to have my own room. Maybe it would make me feel a little more at home there.

He laughed as I hugged him tight. I think it made him feel good to see me so excited.

"Anything for my little girl," he said. "Let's go in so you can see it from the inside."

We went in and looked at it. The walls were still bare studs with electrical wire running through them. It definitely was not pretty, but it was a start. I was so excited to know that I would soon have my own room at dad's house. I would actually have a little privacy there and a room to go to sleep in. It was going to be great!

Dad and I spent most of the evening working outside. He worked on finishing the roof, and I cleaned up the yard. Man, the yard was such a mess! Lindy came out and helped for a few minutes but ended up back in the house. I was glad when she excused herself to go in and make supper.

Dad and I were making pretty good progress. We stopped just long enough to eat supper and went right back to it. We were working pretty hard until dark. We were both tired by the time we were done.

Dad was hoping to finish most of the outside, but we still had quite a bit to do. The good part was the roof was finished, and the yard was looking much better. We talked about plans for the room most of the night.

It was such a good feeling to know I would soon have my very own room here. I hated having to sleep on the couch and having to get dressed in the bathroom. I just had no privacy at dad's and no place to really call my own. Once I have a bedroom, I will feel so much better. I might actually feel like I belong here.

The next morning, we were up early and working outside again. Dad worked on getting the walls ready for siding this time, and I picked up the yard some more.

He finished preparing for the siding but didn't put the siding up. He said he would start it after work on Monday. He started helping me get the yard straightened up. We burned some stuff and bagged other things until it was all finished. It was finally clean! Well, kind of clean.

Dad wanted to start doing stuff on the inside of the room. He put the electrical boxes in and wired everything up. I watched him intently as he worked his way around the whole room.

Lindy made us grilled cheese for lunch. It was my kind of food. After lunch, we all went to the store to get drywall insulation and nails. It was the first time I was ever excited to shop for construction materials. After all, it was for my room.

When we returned home me and dad went straight to work on the insulation. We really worked hard at getting the walls ready for drywall. Dad's friends were coming over tomorrow to help drywall so it had to be done.

The next morning, a few of dad's friends stopped in to help set up the drywall. The insulation wasn't quite done, so they finished that first, and began to drywall. They worked really fast with all of them together. I cleaned things up as they cut drywall and hung it. By the end of the day, the drywall was hung.

We stood back and looked around the room. It looked great! I was so excited!

We didn't stop all weekend. We were so exhausted by evening. We sat down in front of the TV and all fell asleep both nights.

I didn't have school this week because it was spring break, so I stayed an extra few days at Dad's. I ended up going to the grocery store with Lindy Monday morning. I definitely was not excited about going with her, but dad was at work, and I didn't want to stay home by myself. She took me to the consignment shop on the way to get groceries. We found some pretty awesome stuff in there. She bought me a white porcelain jewelry box for my room. It was really fancy looking with the curved legs and everything. It had a light pink rose that was raised up on the top and had leaves and vines going around the box. It was so pretty. She bought me a few figurines, too. I ended up having a pretty good time with her, even though the grocery store was terribly boring.

We finally got home, put away the groceries and went straight to work on my room. We mudded the drywall the best we could. I tried to mud the seams, but I had a pretty hard time getting it to be smooth. Lindy had to go over what I did because it looked so bad.

She was pretty good at mudding. After a few attempts, I resorted to just mudding the nail holes while Lindy did the seams.

When dad got home, he went straight to work on the siding. He did quite a bit before supper. After supper, he hung the door. I went into my room and closed the door. I kept walking around, trying to picture it all finished. I was so happy to know I would have my own room very soon. No more sofa. My thoughts were interrupted by a knock at the door. Dad opened the door and came in. I looked at him and grinned.

"Not too bad, Huh?" he asked.

"Nope, it's great!" I exclaimed as I hugged him. "Thanks, dad. I love it!"

He leaned down and hugged me back. He said, "I'm glad you like it."

He pulled me back and looked at me. He asked, "So, how did things go while I was at work?"

"Okay," I said as I looked around the room again. He asked, "Are you sure?" as he peered at me.

I looked at him with a puzzled look. Then it hit me. He wondered if Lindy and I were getting along.

I replied to him, "We're fine, Dad. Don't worry."

He nodded his head and gave me a squeeze on my shoulder.

Lindy was the least of my problems now that mom had a boyfriend. I didn't even realize it until now, but Lindy and I didn't argue even one time all weekend. We were getting along just fine. I guess I forgot about how much I resented her.

Tuesday, Lindy and I did some more mudding in my room. We worked on it the best we could, but the ceiling had to wait. Dad said he would do that part. It was way too hard!

I was in my room admiring it again when dad came home from work. He knocked on my door and came in.

I went over and gave him a hug. "I thought you were going to be home at five o'clock," I inquired.

"Well, I thought I would come home early since I would rather be here with you," he said as he gave me a smile.

I was really glad he came home early. We both stood there and looked around the room.

"So, do you want to go for a ride?" he asked. "Right now?" I questioned.

"Yes, right now," he replied. "Where are you going?" I asked.

"Oh, just a little ride," he said in an amusing tone. "Sure," I replied, wondering what he was up to.

Soon, we were out of the house and on the road. I was kind of disappointed when I realized Lindy was going, too, but I tried not to show it. I wondered where we were heading to. Dad and Lindy were both acting kind of funny like they had a big secret or something.

We ended up at the hardware store. We picked out paint and carpet for my room. It took a long time for the carpet. It seemed like it took forever to get it ordered. When we finally left, I felt relieved. I was really getting tired of being in the store.

I thought we were headed back home, but I realized we were going in the wrong direction. Dad must have turned when I wasn't paying attention.

"Where are we going?" I asked as I looked around to see where we were.

Nobody answered me. They just looked at each other. I asked again, wondering what was going on.

Dad finally answered, "Oh, just for a drive."

I wondered what they were planning. I watched the road intensely, trying to figure out what they had up their sleeves. Dad pulled into a small parking lot. I thought he was going to turn around at first, but he pulled in and parked.

I looked around, and my heart leaped for joy! It was a furniture store! Dad turned off the truck, and I squealed with excitement. I looked at Dad and then at Lindy. They were both looking back at me with big smiles on their faces.

"So, are you ready to pick out your bedroom outfit?" dad asked as he hooked his keys on his belt loop.

"Yes, Yes, Yes!" I said as I hugged him. I was so excited! What a great weekend I was having. Lindy got out, and I jumped out of the truck and ran to the store.

I heard them laughing as I stood at the door, waiting for them.

We went in and looked at all the possibilities. It took me forever to pick one out. Lindy tried to help by making suggestions since I was having such a hard time.

"What about this one, Samantha? It will match the light pink paint you picked out," Lindy inquired.

I smiled big and said, "It would match perfectly."

It was a canopy bed with very light pink drapes over it. The dressers were white with light pink roses on the drawers. They reminded me of the little jewelry box Lindy just bought me the other day. There was also a white vanity table with matching designs. It was all so beautiful! And not cheap either. When I looked at the price, I wondered if it was too much.

I looked at dad and asked him if it was too expensive. He assured me it was not too much. He told me if I wanted it, then it is mine.

"This is the one," I said as I pointed my finger to the canopy bed. I nodded my head and said, "Yep, this is mine!"

I was so thrilled to have a brand-new bedroom outfit. They told the salesman what they wanted and paid for it. They said it would be delivered in two weeks.

We piled into the pickup and headed home. I felt so lucky to have a father like I have! Some of my friends have dads who don't even care to see them. Some kids don't even know their father. Boy, am I glad my dad cares about me! I didn't think he even cared about me when he first left mom, but now I know he really does care about me and loves me.

We went to a restaurant and ate dinner. It ended up being such an awesome day.

That evening mom called to talk to me. I suddenly had a fierce desire to see her. I really missed her a lot, but I didn't realize it until she called. We didn't talk all week and hearing her voice made me feel so homesick. Funny how that works.

When I hung up the phone, I asked dad if I could go home and see mom. I told him how much I missed her and how homesick I was.

He said, "Of course you can." After about an hour, he ruffled my hair and asked, "Should we get you home?"

I smiled and nodded my head.

He stood up and stretched. "Well, get your stuff ready. I'll be in the garage cleaning up." Dad always liked to be out in his garage. I think it's a man thing. He will say he is going out to clean up, but he is just out there fidgeting with his tools. I think his garage is his place to relax and get time to himself.

I gathered my things as quickly as possible. I couldn't wait to tell mom about my bedroom and the beautiful bedroom set. I was getting butterflies in my stomach just thinking about telling her. She will be so happy for me. It has been a long time since we really talked. I really missed her.

Chapter Nine

Feeling Left Out

When we pulled into the driveway, my eyes were glued to the front door. I waited to see mom pop out of the house. She always came out to the front porch to greet me when dad brought me home. Dad turned off the truck and I sat there a minute waiting and wondering where she was.

Then I remembered she had been working out back in the flower bed lately. That's probably where she was. She will be coming out any minute. Dad's truck is kind of loud, so I know she would have heard him pull in.

Dad jumped out and grabbed my things out of the truck. I slowly opened the door and got out. I finally decided she must not be coming out and walked toward the front door with dad. It kind of hurt my feelings that she didn't come out to greet me. Dad set my things down just inside the door and gave me a hug goodbye.

Just then, mom came through the back door. She must have been in the flower bed, just as I had thought. She must have heard the truck pull in if she was outside. I couldn't understand why she didn't come out front to greet me.

I shook off the hurt feelings and ran to hug her. I excitedly started telling her about the room that dad was building. She stopped hugging me and held out the palms of her hands like a crossing guard.

"Wait, wait, wait…" She said as she shook her head. She paused for silence and continued, "What are you talking about, Sam? Slow down so I can't understand you."

Dad cut in and told me he should get going. I hugged and kissed him as I thanked him for everything he did for me this past week.

As he walked out the door, I walked over and gave mom another big hug.

I started, "I missed you so much! Oh, mom, I had such a great time! Dad is building a room for me. We spent all week working on it. The walls are up, and it looks so cool! We went to the store and…"

At that moment, the sliding glass door opened. I stopped abruptly. We both looked over, and there stood the one person I didn't want to see…Carl. I looked back and forth from mom to Carl a few times, not knowing how to react. It seemed this was happening more and more in my life.

Carl just stood there leaning against the door. "HI, Samantha! How are you?" he asked as he smiled big. He took a good look at me. He must have seen the disgusted look on my face because he quietly slipped back out the door with a wave and a nod.

Mom and I looked at each other. We didn't say a word but knew what the other was thinking. I rolled my eyes. No wonder she wasn't outside to greet me. She was out back, keeping her eyes on someone else. I felt deceived.

Why wouldn't she have told me he was here? Her eyes were pleading with me not to be angry. I could tell she thought I would make a scene again. I decided I should just gather my things and take them to my room instead. I went over and picked up my suitcase. She silently nodded toward me, and out the back door she went. I slowly walked to my room, thinking about how we would eventually lose our close relationship because of Carl.

The following week, I felt pretty glum. Mom wasn't home twice when I got home from school. I knew she was with Carl. It wasn't fair. I didn't even get a chance to tell her about my bedroom set.

One time, I came home from school and sat down to watch some TV. Mom was in her room doing something. Just when I sat down, there was a knock at the door. I went to answer it. To my disappointment, it was Carl. He seemed so fidgety and uncomfortable that he made me feel awkward as well. I walked back to her bedroom door and called out to her, "Mom, Carl's here!"

"Tell him I will be there in a minute!" she called through the door.

I really didn't want to go back out there. It was just way too uncomfortable. I walked very slowly, hoping she would come out before I got out there.

"She'll be out in a minute. She's in her room. I guess she's freshening up a little.," I said as I looked down at my feet.

We stood there for a few long minutes, looking at each other in terrible silence. I started getting nervous and didn't know what to say or do. I searched for something, anything to say, but stood there speechless. Carl kept shifting from one foot to another. I could tell he was really uncomfortable. He acted like he didn't belong here, and he really didn't. Then it dawned on me he wanted me to invite him in!

"Oh," I said, "Come on in."

"Why thank you!" he said as he took off his shoes and followed me into the living room. I sat on the loveseat, and he sat on the sofa. There was another long period of silence, but it was nowhere near as uncomfortable as earlier. At least the TV was on, so I could turn my attention to that. I wished mom would hurry up.

Finally, she came out and WOW! Did she ever look beautiful! Her hair was neatly pinned up, and she had a navy blue sparkly dress on. It was slim fitting and made her look like a superstar. The dress came down to just above her knees, making her legs look long and sleek. Boy, do I hope I look like her when I get older! She was the most beautiful woman in the world.

All the tension left Carl as soon as mom came out. Carl stood up and kissed mom's hand. How flattering. He twirled her around by her hand and told her how beautiful she was.

"Awe, thank you, Carl," she said as she gave him that beautiful smile of hers.

I wanted to tell her how beautiful she looked, but she seemed so flattered by Carl that I figured she probably wouldn't even hear me. She was so in tune with Carl that I didn't even think she knew I was there. I mean, she was even giggling like a schoolgirl.

They sat down on the couch together and started talking. I was feeling very uncomfortable because they weren't even acknowledging I was there. I sat there, feeling invisible, like I was a nobody. The longer they talked, the worse I felt. Finally, I couldn't stand it any longer. I jumped up off the loveseat and stormed off to my room.

"Samantha, where are you going?" I heard mom call out as I walked out of the room.

But it was too late. I didn't want to hear from her. I continued to my room and slammed the door behind me. I threw myself across the bed and cried. My guess was right. I really was going to lose mom to Carl. He could just have her all to himself, and I would just live in my room. I despised him for taking her away. I wished he would just go away and never come back. I wanted mom to love me, not him or anyone else. Besides, I needed mom, and he didn't even need her.

I secretly hoped mom would come in to see what was wrong with me. That way, I would at least know she cared. I waited as I cried and listened for her to walk down the hall. The longer I waited, the worse I felt. Maybe she really didn't care.

By the time she finally came in, I had stopped crying. I was lying on my back blankly, staring at the ceiling. She tried to talk to me but I just ignored her. I pretended she wasn't there, just like she treated me in the living room.

Suddenly, I heard Carl say, "Sharon, it's getting late."

"I'm coming!" she called out. She sat on the edge of my bed and said, "Carl and I are going out for dinner, and I would love it if you would come too."

I knew she didn't plan on me tagging along. It was obvious by the way she was dressed. She would have told me to get ready if she planned on me joining them. I wanted to go so bad but I knew they didn't want me to go. Besides, I couldn't go dressed in jeans and a T-shirt. Mom looked too dressed up for me to go in regular clothes.

I continued to stare at the ceiling, trying so hard not to respond to her. She gave up and walked to the door. She paused and turned toward me.

She spoke in a cold tone, "There's burritos in the freezer. You can pop it in the microwave when you get hungry. We'll be back in a few hours. Love you, Samantha."

She stood there for a few seconds, waiting for me to reply. I wanted to go so bad. My insides were pleading for mom to grab me and hug me, to tell me to get ready and that I was going whether I wanted to or not. But she walked out of my room, closing the door behind her.

I went to my window and watched them walk to Carl's car. My heart yearned for mom. Suddenly, I didn't care how I was dressed. I wanted to go with them. I ran out of my room and out to the front porch. They were backing out of the driveway as I ran down the steps, waving my arms and yelling to get their attention. They didn't even look my way. They just drove off down the road. I stood there feeling empty and alone. It bummed me out so bad.

I slowly walked back into the house, feeling sorry for myself. I spent the next three hours moping around the house doing nothing. It was the longest three hours of my life. The more time I had to think about it, the sadder I became. They were probably glad I didn't go. Mom only asked me because she knew I was mad about being left out. It was all out of pity for me, anyway.

Finally, I heard someone pull into the driveway. I peeked out of the living room window. It was mom and Carl. I ran to my bedroom as fast as I could. Although I was happy mom was home, I was still angry, and I wanted to make sure she knew it. That was one thing I was really good at...giving her guilt trips. The great thing about that was mom always fell for it. She would feel bad and spoil me rotten! That's the part I loved.

Mom came into my room after a few minutes. I decided to pretend like I was sleeping. That way, she would know how bored I was while she was gone. She walked over to me and ran her fingers through my hair. She bent down and gave me a kiss on the forehead, and left the room. It made me feel happy the way she did that. It really felt like she loved me and cared about me. Even though she thought I was sleeping, she was still as sweet as could be toward me. It made me wonder if she did that all the time while I really was sleeping. I felt pretty lucky to have her as a mom, even though I was still trying to hold a grudge against her.

After that night, Carl came over almost every evening, and mom just doted over him. I retired to my room early most of the time. I couldn't stand the way she constantly flirted with him. She acted like a high school girl every time he was around. It made me sick.

One night, Martha and her boyfriend came over and had dinner with us. Carl was there, too. I felt pretty out of place with two couples. I went to my room as soon as dinner was over that night. The last thing I wanted was to sit and listen to the flirting and ignorant humor any more than I had to. Martha could be pretty stupid with her wisecracks sometimes.

Chapter Ten

Tricia & Jake

The only relief I got through the week was being at school. No stress there. Jacob has been talking to me quite a bit lately. Every time I respond to him, I always feel like I say the stupidest things. I wish I had the right thing to say, but I always seem to sound so dumb. Oh well, he still talks to me, so I must not sound too bad.

In class I sometimes catch myself just gazing at him. I have to really watch myself because he has already caught me staring at him a few times. I can't help it, though. He is so cute! I love looking at him.

On Friday, Tricia and I sat together at lunchtime like usual. She told me Carrie was coming over for the weekend. She was really excited about it. She was babbling on for a bit, and then she suddenly stopped mid-sentence and looked at me. I started to laugh because she looked so funny the way she did it.

"I know, I was rambling," she said as she shrugged her shoulders.

"All you needed was a light bulb over your head," I said between the giggles.

She started laughing, too. We joked about how silly she looked.

"Seriously, we are going to the drive-in on Saturday. Think your mom will let you come?" she asked.

I was chewing my food, so I held up my finger. "I don't know. I'll ask when I get home."

Tricia smiled, "I hope you can. It'll be so fun!"

I smiled back at her. Yeah, It would be. I really hoped mom would let me go. Then I thought about her mom. I asked, "Will your mom care if I come too?"

"Nah, she likes you," Tricia replied as she shook her head.

I really wanted to go to the movies with Tricia and Carrie. I hoped mom didn't have anything planned for Saturday. I wanted to ask her right away so she wouldn't make plans or anything. But, of course, I was disappointed to come home to an empty house again. It really sucks. I wasted time painting my nails, hoping mom would get home soon.

The phone rang. It was Tricia. "So, what did your mom say? Can you go?" she asked.

I told her she wasn't even home, and I would call her when I found out.

A few hours later, mom finally came home and guess who she brought with her? The one, the only, Carl. I was a little irritated, but I had to be on my best behavior. I wanted to go to Tricia's, and I knew mom wouldn't let me if I started acting up. I really wanted to be mean, though. I just bit my tongue over and over again.

Carl kept asking me question after question about how my day went. It was really getting on my nerves. After about five minutes, he gave a little pause. I jumped at the opportunity and asked mom if I could go to Tricia's to stay overnight on Saturday.

She said yes. I was so glad.

It was always so much fun at Tricia's. Her mom always takes us places. She will take us to the movies, the mall, wherever we want to go. She's always so nice.

By Saturday late morning, I packed up my things, and mom drove me to Tricia's. Mom lectured me all the way to her house about being on my best behavior. It was like she knew about the magazines or something. My guilt was getting the best of me. She kept going on and on about how she found herself in predicaments when she was young due to peer pressure. Strange how she would pick this time to talk to me about how to handle bad situations. The more she talked, the guiltier I felt. I was afraid she would see it on my face, so I stared out the passenger window the whole time. I made sure I didn't look at her.

Tricia and Carrie came running out to the car when we pulled into the driveway. Mom gave me a peck on the cheek and reminded me one more time to be good.

"I will, love you," I said and hugged her.

I jumped out of the car and took my bags from the back seat. Tricia grabbed one of my bags, and the girls escorted me to the house. We took my stuff to Tricia's room and sat in there chatting for a little while.

I was really hoping the magazines weren't going to come out again after mom made me feel so guilty. Besides, looking at them made me feel bad.

We spent our time picking through Tricia's closet for the perfect outfits to wear to the movies. We were all pretty much the same size, and Tricia had so many cool clothes. I loved wearing her clothes.

We went through her jewelry box and picked out necklaces for each of us. We were in the middle of makeup when Tricia's mom called us for supper. We really had to hurry it up, then. By the second call for supper, we were ready to go. We ate and off we went to the movies.

The best part of the drive-in is the concession stand. That is where everyone hangs out. We always find excuses to go there at least a few times to see who's there. We never stay long because Tricia's mom won't let us. She always tells us to get right back when we are done getting our food or our drinks. She knows we want to hang out there. After all, who needs to make three or four trips to the concession stand in just a few hours?

The first movie started just as we returned from the concession stand. We talked through the whole movie, giggling and joking around. We hardly saw any of the movie at all. Tricia's mom told us to pipe down a few times. I think she was irritated by how loud we were. Since she knew we weren't even watching the movie, she sent us to the concession stand for a drink. I think she wanted a few minutes of peace and quiet.

As we stood at the end of the line, the people in front of us turned around, and oh wow, it was Jake! He and his friend Tim were right in front of us! Tricia noticed him, and her face lit right up as she looked over at me. She nudged me, then motioned for me to say something, but I just stood there frozen. I started to blush. I could feel my face getting redder and redder.

Once she realized I wasn't going to say anything, Tricia took matters into her own hands. "Hi Jake, how ya doin?" she said, all giddy.

Carrie looked at him, then looked at me with her mouth wide open. She smiled at me, and I knew I was in trouble. At that moment, I regretted telling them who I liked. My heart sank to my stomach, and I started to tremble. I began to sway as my legs felt like rubber bands.

Jake replied to Tricia, "Hey." He turned toward me and nodded. I nodded back.

The girls both turned around and put their hands over their mouths simultaneously. They were getting a kick out of this, and here I was, wishing I could disappear. I worried about what they were going to do or say. They both started giggling, which made Jake and Tim look back at us again. By then, I could feel that my face was on fire from embarrassment.

Tricia and Carrie whispered and giggled the whole time we were in line. Jake and Tim kept turning around to look at them. They made such a spectacle of us! I just wanted to crawl into a hole somewhere and hide.

All of a sudden, I heard, "Hi, Samantha!"

I turned around and there stood Franky and Harold. This was the worst! I looked over at Jake, hoping he didn't notice. Of course, he was looking straight at me. I could have had a heart attack right then and there!

Franky is the boy that sits next to me in English class. He is kind of gross. He is a bit on the heavy side, which isn't bad, but what makes it bad is that he runs around begging everybody for their lunch. There were a few times when a bunch of kids got together to see how much he could eat. They all gave him their lunch and chanted as he ate it all as fast as he could. It made me sick to see him engulfed in food as everybody circled around him. He didn't even understand what a fool he was making of himself. I think he loved the attention, but it wasn't good attention they were giving him.

Anyway, he always tries to talk to me during class. I hate the way everyone is so mean to him, so I talk to him some. I try to keep it short because I can tell he has a crush on me. I am by far not mean to him. I just try not to be super nice to him on purpose because I don't want him to think I like him in that way. Everyone is so mean to him, though, that just being nice gives him the wrong message.

I looked at Jake, hoping he wouldn't judge me over being friends with Franky. I turned around and nodded toward Franky without saying a word. I didn't want Jake to think I was too friendly with him.

Tricia and Carrie both looked at me and cringed their faces. Carrie was bold enough to act like she was gagging herself with her finger. I grabbed her hand away and shook my head. I didn't want to be mean to Franky or Harold. I just didn't want to be seen talking to them when Jake was right in front of me.

When we finished up in line, we started back to the car. Jake and Tim stepped out in front of us. We stopped and screamed, startled and speechless. We all laughed as I wondered what they wanted.

Jake spoke up, "Hey, we were wondering if you guys wanted to hang out with us up here." He looked at me the whole time he spoke. It seemed like his eyes were piercing right through me. He never looked at me that way before. My heart started pounding out of my chest.

I started to speak, but all I could do was stutter. I knew Tricia's mom wouldn't let us stay up there and hang out the rest of the night.

Tricia saved me by blurting out, "Sure, Why not?"

I couldn't believe she said that! Tricia's mom would be up here looking for us in no time. I didn't want to go through that embarrassment in front of these guys.

It took about five minutes to figure out that Tim liked Tricia. He was giving all his attention to her. He tried to get her away from us so he could talk to her alone, but we kept her right beside us. We weren't about to let her out of our sight.

Jake acted strange at first, but after a few minutes he clearly started flirting with me. I was soaking it all in! I liked him a lot, and it felt so good to get some attention from him. He never showed this kind of interest before. It was really the best day of my life! I had butterflies in my stomach, and I was loving every second of it!

It didn't take but fifteen minutes before Tricia's mom came storming through the crowd, looking for us. Tricia saw her first and grabbed mine and Carrie's arms.

"Excuse us, we have to go," she said as she pulled us away quickly.

She guided us away from the boys. I looked back and held my free arm up to wave at Jake as we quickly snuck away.

Tricia guided us to the bathroom and told us, "My mom's out there looking for us. Act like we've been here the whole time."

Just as she finished warning us, her mom walked in. She put her hands on her hips and said, "There you guys are! I've been looking everywhere for you."

Tricia jumped in, "The line was really long, and we had to wait in line for the restroom too." She rolled her eyes and added, "We've been waiting forever!" She sounded so believable. She was a good liar, that was for sure.

I only hoped her mom wouldn't look at me. I was a dead giveaway. I was shaking from nervousness. A woman came out of one of the stalls, and I swiftly ran in to hide. It gave me a few minutes to calm down a bit and kept me from Tricia's mom. One look at me would have made her suspicious. Besides, I needed to use the bathroom anyway.

We all walked back to the car and finished what little was left of the movie. We stayed up most of the night talking about the boys we hung out with at the movies.

I was so bummed out when mom pulled into the driveway first thing in the morning. She was all excited about a big day she planned. I looked forward to it until she mentioned Carl was coming, too. Once I heard that, I stopped listening.

She was rambling on and would stop every now and then to say, "Did you hear me?" I would nod my head even if I didn't hear her. I had no interest in hanging out with Carl all day.

Besides, I was too busy thinking about Jake and how cute he was. Carrie and Tricia both said they could tell that he liked me. Is it true? Does he really like me?

"Samantha, what are you doing?" mom chimed in, leering at me.

Oops, she knew I didn't hear a word she said. She drove home silently the rest of the way. When we pulled into the driveway, I noticed Carl's car was there. No big surprise. At least he doesn't park at Martha's to sneak over anymore.

We ended up going to the mall. Carl actually bought me a few things. I guess it was nice of him, but I could have gone without. We went out to eat afterward. It was kind of awkward. Carl was talking and talking. I think he felt the tension, and it made him nervous or something. He just rambled on and on. He wouldn't shut up.

That night mom came into my room to tuck me in. She didn't do that very often anymore. I started to get the hint after a while. The only time she would tuck me in anymore was when she wanted to talk to me about something. Usually, it was, yes, of course, about Carl.

She sat on the side of my bed and began, "Samantha, you really need to stop being so cold toward Carl. He really likes you and wants to be a part of your life, too."

Here it goes…I rolled on my side to get away from her and pulled the covers up to my neck.

Her tone sharpened, "I mean it, Samantha. I can see how cold you are toward him. He is a nice guy if you would just give him a chance."

I sighed and said robotically, "OK, Mom." Whatever would have been a more meaningful reply but I knew those would be fighting words. I didn't even feel like fighting right then.

I was getting pretty tired of mom trying to make me like Carl. He might be nice to me, but he was taking my mom away from me. He was invading my life. I never get any time with mom anymore because he is always right in between us. How am I supposed to like someone who puts a wedge between me and the person I love most?

She finally gave up, kissed me on the top of my head, said goodnight and left. I was relieved when she left. My mind turned to Jake as I drifted off to sleep.

The following week, Jake talked to me more than usual. He even looked at me differently. I wondered what was up but just let it go. I liked the change in him. By Wednesday he asked me for my phone number. I was so excited! I couldn't wait to tell Tricia. The day seemed so long I just couldn't stand it. The last bell finally rang, and I ran out of the classroom and straight to my locker. I knew Tricia would be there waiting for me since her last class was right next to my locker.

"He just asked me for my number!" I exclaimed as I put my hands up in victory.

"Who? Jake?" She asked as her eyes lit up. "Yes!" I screeched as I tried to contain myself.

She did a little victory dance and said, "See, I told you he liked you."

By the time we finished talking about it, we both had to run to the buses. The bus started moving right when we reached the door. The bus driver stopped and opened the door for us. He told us to get here sooner next time as he grumbled under his breath.

"Sorry," I said as we jumped on the bus. Everybody oohed and aahed as we walked down the aisle. I found a seat as fast as I could to take the attention away from me.

I went home and pretty much waited for the phone to ring. I really expected a call from Jake that night. I just couldn't wait! Every time the phone rang, my heart would skip a beat.

I felt pretty disappointed when I started to get ready for bed. There was no way Jake was going to call now. Just as I pulled on my nightgown, the phone rang. I paused, closed my eyes and said a little "Please, God, let it be Jake" prayer. I knew this was the last shot to be able to talk to him tonight.

Mom called out, "Samantha, you have a phone call."

I ran to the kitchen and grabbed the phone. My heart was beating so fast it hurt. I paused for a few seconds, gathered myself and said, "Hello."

"Well, did he call?" I let out a breath. It was Tricia. I was so bummed. I felt like crying but knew it would do no good. We talked a little while. She assured me he would probably call me tomorrow.

Mom eventually popped into the kitchen and motioned for me to hang up the phone. I nodded as I told Tricia I had to go.

The rest of the week, Jake and I talked in class, but that was it. I waited all week for him to call. I was very disappointed each night that I didn't hear from him. I finally figured out that he just wasn't going to call me at all. It really bummed me out, but at least he talked to me at school all the time now.

Chapter Eleven

My Room

The weekend came, and it was time to go to dad's house. I packed my things as soon as I got home from school. Mom was nowhere in sight, as usual. I took my suitcase to the living room, sat it down and called dad to see when he was coming. He said he was on his way and would be here in ten minutes. I told him that sounded great. I couldn't wait to see my room. I wondered what it looked like now. I didn't know if it was done or not, but I didn't care. It was my own bedroom, and that alone made me thrilled.

I gave my dad a big hug and smiled from ear to ear when he got here. It felt nice to see him. I was glad at least one parent wanted to see me.

"Where's your mother?" he asked as he scoped the front porch.

"I don't know. She isn't home much," I said as I shrugged my shoulders.

"Think we should try to get a hold of her, so she knows you are with me?" He asked.

"Nah, I left a note on the fridge," I said as I thought about how she used to leave notes for me, but not anymore. She just didn't seem to care much at all now. All she cared about was being with Carl.

When dad and I walked into the house, I was immediately greeted by Lindy. She came right up to me and gave me a squeeze. It really surprised me. She stood there looking at me with a great big grin on her face. I wondered what she was thinking about. She looked kind of stupid standing there with a great big grin from ear to ear.

Thinking about it made me want to laugh, but I surprisingly held it in. Finally, I couldn't stand it any longer.

"What are you smiling so big for?" I asked as I raised my eyebrows and smiled back.

"Come on," Lindy said as she grabbed my arm. She made me close my eyes as she practically dragged me toward my new room. She stopped and placed her hands on my shoulders.

"Open your eyes!" she exclaimed with excitement.

I looked around with my mouth wide open. I was astonished by what I saw. The carpet was white, the walls were painted a very light pink with pink floral wall decals, and the ceiling fan was white. It was completely finished!

Even the beautiful bedroom set was there. I stood there a moment, giving myself time to soak it all in. I looked at Lindy and dad with my mouth still wide open. They both laughed light-heartedly as I hugged each of them.

I told them how much I loved it and thanked them a hundred times. I found out that Lindy did all the painting and decorating. She was finishing it up when dad came to get me. She wanted to get it done to surprise me.

"Oh, I am surprised!" I said as I raised my arms up. "Thank you, Lindy. Thank you so much! It looks beautiful, and I love it!" I exclaimed as I gave her another hug.

"Awe, I am so glad you like it," She said as she kissed my cheek.

I looked around the room and noticed my jewelry box sitting on my dresser. I went over and opened it up. It was so pretty. I just loved it. It matched my room perfectly! I went to get my things so

I could put them away. I actually had a dresser now! No more living out of suitcases and duffle bags. I stayed in my room most of the evening, just enjoying the privacy I had. Dad and Lindy popped in every so often to talk to me. I really loved my room. I wished I could just stay in it forever, but I could tell Dad wanted me to come out and visit with them.

I went to the living and dad was sitting on the couch, all hunched up. I sat down next to him. Lindy was sitting at her sewing table. I noticed a doll on the desk next to her. It perked my curiosity, so I jumped up to get a better look. The doll only had an upper body. The cloth she was working on was white satin.

"Watcha doin?" I asked.

"I am making a doll for your bed," said Lindy while she sewed a hem in the cloth.

I lit up as I asked, "You mean the ones with long fancy dresses?" "Yeah, it will spread out in a circle on your bed," she replied.

I smiled as I pictured it all finished, sitting on my bed. It made me feel honored she would take the time to do something like that for me. I mean, she already did a lot of hard work in my room.

"Can I help?" I asked in a small voice, not sure how much help I could actually be. I knew nothing about sewing.

"Sure," she said as she fidgeted through a box of pearls and little decorations. She took out a light pink bow and handed it to me. Put this in her hair and pick out some jewelry for her," she said as she picked up the box and held it out to me.

I sat on the couch next to dad, and he helped me pick out jewelry for my doll. We worked on the doll together all that night and started back up in the morning. Dad eventually went out to the garage while me and Lindy busied ourselves on our little project. We were so indulged in it that neither one of us heard dad come in.

"How are ya's coming along?" Dad asked as he leaned against the archway. Lindy and I both jumped and looked at him in surprise. How long had he been there? We were so engulfed in what we were doing we didn't even know he was there.

Lindy put her hand on her heart and said, "Hunny, you startled me.." I added, "Me too, dad. I didn't even hear you come in."

"I'm just watching the two most important girls in my life," He said with a look of contentment on his face. His eyes seemed to sparkle with the zest of life as he stood there, looking so handsome and happy.

Lindy and I both smiled at him. All at once, he lost our attention as we both got back to work on what we were doing.

"Mind if I run to the lumber yard for paint while you two are busy?" dad asked. "I really need to paint that shed out back. It looks terrible, and I can't stand it anymore," he explained.

"Okay," Lindy said, not even looking up. "We'll see you in a bit."

Dad walked over to her and gave her a kiss on the cheek. He walked over to me and did the same. He whispered in my ear, "You okay with that?"

I nodded my head and went back to work on the doll. I think he really came in planning to take me along with him. He always took me everywhere he went, since Lindy and I had a history of not getting along. She has been so much better lately. I think I might even be starting to like her a little bit.

He turned to walk out the door. He called out, "See you two beautiful women in an hour or so."

We both hollered bye and continued working on the doll. By one o'clock, Dad came back. Lindy and I picked up our sewing mess and made a quick lunch. We ate together at the table and talked about my room, dad's work and Lindy's sewing projects.

Dad stood up and said he had to get outside and start painting the shed. I asked if I could help. Lindy went into her closet and found an old shirt for me to wear. We went out to get started while Lindy cleaned up lunch.

One thing I discovered is that Dad is a very messy painter. Now I know why Lindy painted my room. He was splashing paint all over the place and it ended up dripping in my hair. I painted his arm to get back at him, and soon, we were in a paint fight.

Lindy was walking out to us at the time. She tried to stop us at first, but dad grabbed her by the cheeks with his paint-filled hands and gave her a great big kiss.

Lindy had dad's hand prints on her cheeks. It was so funny. She kind of giggled, took a paintbrush, dipped it in paint and flung it at dad. The paint splattered him all over his shirt. It was so fun to play in paint like this with two adults. We ended up with an awful lot of painted grass and completely ruined clothes. We really had a blast painting the shed in the end.

Of course, nobody could wait to take a shower when we finished. We stood in line in the kitchen, just waiting for our turn. The paint feels so gross when it dries on you.

Sunday morning, we started on the bed doll again. We worked on it all morning and into the afternoon. It really was nice to spend time with Lindy. It felt really good to be on the same page for a change. By late afternoon, we had finally finished the doll. We sat her on the bed and stood back to admire our work. She looked so beautiful, it was breathtaking. Just the touch my room needed.

She had long, wavy blonde hair. The sides of her hair were pulled back by the light pink ribbon Lindy gave me. Her sleeves were puffy with miniature light pink bows around the cuffs. Her white satin dress flowed in a circle around her. Lindy attached little light pink bows and ribbons to the outskirt of her dress. She had a pink ribbon around her waist with little pink roses. She was gorgeous! She was just as fancy as my canopy bed was… perfect match!

"Thanks, Lindy. She's breathtaking," I said as I gazed at her.

Lindy smiled as she looked at the doll lying on my bed. "She is, isn't she?" I went outside to get dad so I could show him the doll. Sure enough, he was in his garage tinkering with a circuit board. He had a knack for electronics.

I went in and pulled his arm as I said, "Come on, dad. She's all done. She looks so beautiful on my bed. You have to come to see her."

"Okay, just a sec," he said as he finished placing a transmitter on the circuit board. We came in and looked at her. He told us we did a great job on her, and off he went out to the garage again. Lindy and I just stood there, looking at each other and shaking our heads. Guys…they just don't understand.

At two o'clock, the phone rang. It was mom! "Hey, is everything okay?" I asked. She rarely called when I was at dad's for just the weekend. I thought maybe something was wrong.

"Oh, everything is fine. Is your dad around?" she asked.

"Just a second," I said as I laid the phone down and ran to the garage.

"Dad, mom's on the phone!" I called out as I peeked my head in the door.

"Okay, I'm coming," he said as he glanced my way.

I ran back in and picked up the phone. I talked to her for a while until dad came in. He took the phone and was quiet for a long moment. I sat there, waiting to hear what was up. I knew something was going on.

Suddenly, dad sounded mad. He said, "Wait a minute, this is my time."

"NO," dad said as he was shaking his head. "No, that's not okay," he said.

I knew he was really mad and wondered if I should escape to my room.

"I don't care, you have her all week." dad said in an irritated voice. Another pause.

I knew I should leave, but I couldn't tear myself away.

"Sharon, I have two days. Yes, I know I was late a few times. Listen to me, I have... Sharon, don't start!" Dad said, raising his voice.

"Okay, Yes, I understand, but it's my time... Yes, okay. Bye," Dad sighed as he hung up the phone.

I sat there looking at him. I wondered if I should ask what was going on or not. He looked pretty irritated. He looked up at me and put on a fake smile. I think he just realized I heard everything he said.

"Sorry you had to hear that," he said with a sad look.

"It's okay, Dad. Is everything alright?" I cautiously asked. "Yeah, your mom wants you to come home early," he said. "Why?" I questioned.

"I guess she will have to be the one to tell you that," he replied.

For the next half hour, I couldn't get mom out of my mind. I wondered why she would want me to come home early. Was something wrong? It made me kind of anxious to get home. I hoped everything was okay.

"Well, why don't you pack your things and we will get you home," dad said as he rubbed his hand through his hair. He was obviously frustrated. I went to my room and packed quickly. I wanted to get home a soon as possible. I just knew something was wrong.

Mom never did this before. When I came out of my room, dad and Lindy were sitting at the table in deep conversation. They were quietly talking until they noticed me. Suddenly, the conversation stopped. I stood there, looking at them and wondering what was going on. I suddenly felt a deep darkness coming very soon in my life.

"Is there something I should know?" I asked with my voice cracking.

"No, your mom will tell you," Dad said as he got up and put on his shoes. He gave Lindy a quick kiss on the cheek and said, "Let's get going."

So off we went on my way home. Something terrible was about to happen; I just knew it. I had such a bad feeling about all of this. Something was about to happen that would change my life forever.

Chapter Twelve

Engagement

The first thing I saw was Carl's car in the driveway. Great, just who I wanted to see…NOT! Mom wasn't outside waiting for me again. She is the one who wanted me home and she still wouldn't come out to greet me. I guess those days are gone forever. Oh well, I guess I was getting used to it, anyway.

I went in and set my bags down by the front door. I went to the sliding doors to look for mom. I thought she might be out in the backyard.

"Hey," Carl called.

I turned around, startled. There was Carl, sitting on the couch.

"Oh, hey. I didn't know anyone was in here," I said as I turned back to the sliding glass door to look outside for mom again.

"Come in here, Samantha." This time, it was mom's voice. I didn't even see her at first. She was sitting in the rocking chair. I slowly walked into the living room.

"What is going on, Mom?" I asked, scared to really know. "Come sit with us," mom said as she leaned forward in her chair.

I felt strange, but I sat down on the loveseat. We all just sat there, not saying a word. It was a very weird moment. Something was up. I didn't even want to hear it because I knew it was going to be bad news. I could tell by the way they were acting. Unbelievable tension was in the air.

Mom started, "You know, Carl and I have been spending a lot of time together, and we have been discussing things."

My heart started to race. I had a real fear of what was to come. I didn't want to hear it because I had a huge feeling whatever it was would ruin my life. Please don't tell me Carl is moving in. Please, God, I pleaded silently.

"You haven't even had the chance to meet his boys yet. I think it's time you met them," mom finished.

I let out a huge sigh of relief. This, I could handle. "When?" I asked.

"Well, how about now?" mom said with a fake cheery tone. "What?" I asked, shocked.

"We are going to take a ride over to Carl's house. It will give you a chance to meet the boys and to see his house, too," mom said.

This is not what I expected at all. I have been gone all weekend, and now I have to spend the rest of the day elsewhere, hanging out with people I don't even care to know.

Mom was saying how it would mean so much to both of them for me to meet his kids. I sighed quietly and hoped they didn't see the misery I felt inside on my face.

I guess mom must have seen it because she scowled at me when Carl wasn't looking. She didn't miss it like I hoped she did.

So, off we went to Carl's house. Just where I never wanted to go. I would have rather stayed at dad's longer. As we pulled into his driveway, I was very impressed. His house was huge and very expensive looking. It was a brick two-story house with a stone chimney on the side. Very classy looking. I was curious what the inside looked like.

As we got out of the car, I took a second to admire the house. It almost looked like a small version of a mansion. It was beautiful.

Suddenly, just when I was dreaming of living in a home like this with mom, the screen door flew open and crashed against the side of the house. Two of the loudest boys I had ever seen came running out full force, yelling and chasing one another. Carl yelled at them about the door as he walked around the vehicle. They showed no sign of hearing him at all. They just kept whooping and hollering as they ran after one another. The taller boy caught hold of the other and took him down. They wrestled on the ground for a bit.

"Okay, That's enough!" Carl yelled with a stern voice. It kind of made me jump. I never heard him yell before.

The boys stopped and looked Carl's way. They saw mom and I and immediately stood up and straightened out their clothes. They stood there quietly, looking like a couple of bums. Their jeans were grass-stained, and their hair looked like they hadn't brushed it in weeks.

Carl waved them over to introduce them to me. As they came closer, I noticed they had dirt all over their faces.

"Boys, this is Samantha. She is Sharon's daughter. Samantha, these are my boys. Taylor and Bradley," Carl said proudly. He seemed so happy to introduce us.

But I was not impressed at all. They were so loud and obnoxious... I just thought they were dumb. After a pause, Carl nodded his head toward his sons as he said, "Boys." There was an edge to his voice.

Taylor caught on right away and put out his hand. He said, "Nice to meet you. I'm Taylor."

I looked at his hand for a split second, wishing I didn't have to touch him. He looked so dirty! I looked him in the face and shook his hand, trying not to think of his dirty hand. I nodded.

Taylor nudged Bradley. He looked up at him in a bewildered way, then put his hand out. His hand was even filthier, and his nails were full of dirt. It was so disgusting!

He said, "Same here, I'm Bradley."

"Thanks," I said for lack of better words. I glanced at mom, hoping I could get out of shaking his hand. Mom nodded her head toward Bradley. I shook his hand and slowly wiped my hand off on my pants. I tried not to make it obvious what I was doing. I was so grossed out!

"Well, let's go in, and I will show you around," Carl said as he walked toward the house. Mom and I followed while the boys went back to wrestling and chasing each other.

Carl showed me around the house, taking me from room to room. The inside of the house was beautiful. The rooms were all so huge! I wondered if he was rich. By the looks of things, I would have to answer yes. His boys' rooms were an absolute mess, but the other rooms were perfect. I figured he must have a maid or something because men do not keep things this clean.

As he finished showing me around upstairs, we suddenly heard a huge ruckus going on downstairs. The door sounded like it slammed off its hinges, and we heard loud, obnoxious voices echoing through the whole house. I looked at Carl with a concerned look. He looked at me and threw his head back as he let out a laugh.

"Boys will be boys. They just don't listen," he said as he put his hand on my shoulder, reassuring me that it would be okay.

As we walked down the stairway, the boys ran carelessly up the stairs and bumped into me.

"Hey, calm down!" Carl yelled as he grabbed my arm to steady me.

I came to the conclusion that Carl had the most beautiful house I had ever seen and the worst boys in the world to go along with it.

We met mom in the kitchen to have a cup of hot chocolate. She already had it ready for us by the time we came downstairs. Carl called the boys down to come join us.

It was strange to sit there and make small talk with two boys who were kicking each other under the table and laughing. Carl finally got mad and yelled at them. It calmed them both down some, thankfully. I could hardly stand them any longer.

I looked over at Carl and noticed he was in deep thought. He wasn't paying attention to any of us. I wondered if he was okay.

Suddenly, his eyes brightened and he said, "Hey guys, let's go in the den and sit for a bit. I have something I want to talk to all of you about." He stood up and swooshed his arms toward the den. We all got up and followed him.

The boys moved past me and plopped on the loveseat. Mom sat in the recliner, and Carl sat on the sofa. There were no other seats available for me. I stood in the middle of the room, feeling awkward and alone. I wondered if I should just sit on the floor.

Carl scooted over and patted the cushion on the couch. I obliged and sat down. It was a bit uncomfortable sitting next to him, but at least I had a place to sit. As we all settled in our seats, the room suddenly became so quiet you could hear a pin drop. Something odd was going on, and we all knew it.

Carl leaned forward, rubbing his hands together nervously. He began, "Uh.. well, you all know Sharon and I have been seeing quite a lot of each other..."

An eerie, long pause developed as we all looked around at each other. Finally, Taylor broke the silence, "And?"

"Well, everything has been going so well with us that we are talking about getting married." Carl looked nervously around, like he was studying our reactions.

The room was even quieter than before, and my heart dropped in pure terror. No way could this be happening. Taylor and Bradley didn't look any happier than I did.

Carl saw our stressed looks and held out his hands. He began, "Not right now, guys. We have just been discussing it and decided we should set a date for the future. I just want you all to know now so you can get used to the idea. You know, like, in a year or so."

Mom cut in, "We just want you kids to know that we really love each other an awful lot. I don't want you kids to be left in the dark about things. We both care about each of you, and we care about your feelings, too."

Carl continued, "Anyway, we are planning on setting a date for next year sometime. It won't happen for a while....."

I didn't hear anything else Carl said. His voice faded out as I thought about them getting married. I couldn't even picture it. It was completely absurd. How could this happen? No way would I have any part in it. I just couldn't. Carl? My stepfather? These wild boys, my step-brothers? Where would we live? Mom's house isn't big enough for all of us. Would we move here? I was sick to my stomach thinking of all these things. I started feeling dizzy from anxiety. I couldn't take it anymore. I stood up and went outside to get some fresh air. Mom followed me out, but I wasn't ready for a chat. I really felt sick.

Mom tried to talk to me, but I couldn't even look at her. I stared off into the distance, not even hearing what she had to say. I think she realized I wasn't ready to talk yet (Nor would I ever be ready to talk) and sat there quietly on the porch rubbing my back. No words were spoken. We just sat there mindlessly looking out at the trees. We sat there for what seemed an eternity. I didn't want to move.

It was peaceful, just mom and I. When I started feeling better, mom finally spoke. She asked me if I was ready to go in. I silently stood up and followed her into the house. I really had to work hard to get myself together.

Taylor and Bradley helped to distract me. They took me upstairs, and we hung out in Taylor's room. I found out they weren't as bad as I thought they were at first. However, they were still loud and obnoxious in my eyes.

Carl finally took us home at eight o'clock. As we walked in the door, I let out a huge sigh of relief. It felt good to be in my own territory again. At least I could be comfortable and be myself. I went to my room just to be around my things. As I closed the door, I heard the phone ringing.

Mom popped her head in the door. "Tricia's on the phone."

I walked over to get the phone from her. I made a huge effort not to look at mom, but I couldn't help it. I glanced at her quickly. Her face used to be a ray of sunshine to me. Now, it's just another face. She really let me down with all of this mess. She was ruining my life, and she knew it.

She pleaded with me in her eyes as she handed me the phone, but I would not give in. I was not going to act like everything was okay.

"Hi," I said as I turned my attention to the phone. "Hey, How was it at your dad's?" Tricia asked.

I forgot all about my room and all the good things that happened there. I was so engrossed in mom and Carl getting engaged that it completely slipped my mind. I was so glad Tricia called. I got to tell her all about my room and the doll Lindy and I made. I also told her about mom wanting to get married to Carl. I had the chance to talk to someone who would take my side, and it felt good to have someone who understands how I feel about everything. I said my goodbyes to Tricia and started to unpack my things from dad's.

Mom popped her head back into my room just as I finished unpacking. "I almost forgot, a boy named Jake called while you were at your dad's," mom said.

"He did?" I asked as I jerked my head toward her. It really caught me by surprise. I was taken aback by the thought that he actually called. My eyes must have been huge because mom just laughed and said something about being all Google-eyed.

"He left his number. It's hanging on the fridge," she said.

I heard mom laughing as I ran past her and headed for the fridge. I was so happy he called! I was all giddy as I looked at the phone number in my hand. I walked back to my room to get the phone. I stared at the paper as I sat on my bed. Did I have enough guts to call him back? What would I say? I didn't think I could do it.

I ended up calling Tricia instead. She squealed with joy and insisted I call him back. We ended up chatting for so long that it was too late to call him by the time I hung up. I was disappointed, but blew it off. I didn't have the guts to call him anyway.

Chapter Thirteen

Trouble Lying in Wait

The next day, I went to class all excited about seeing Jake. I was so into him!

He asked me why I didn't call him back. I told him I got the message too late.

"Hey, do you and Tricia want to go to the drive-in with Tim and me Friday night?" he asked in a matter-of-fact way.

"How will we get there?" I asked.

"My older brother is taking us," he replied.

"Sure, why not?" I said with butterflies in my stomach.

"Cool," Jake said as he gave me that big smile of his. It made my stomach do flip flops thinking about going to the movies with him.

Then I wondered how I would ever get mom to let me go. I was only twelve, soon to be thirteen. Wow, and I didn't even think about my birthday coming up. So much has been happening that it slipped my mind. I wondered if mom would even remember it since she has been so wrapped up in Carl.

I couldn't wait to tell Tricia, but she wasn't on the bus. Her mom must have picked her up today. I'll just have to call her.

When I got home, I put my book bag on the floor next to the front door. I started to walk toward the living room and stopped dead in my tracks as I noticed Carl sitting on the sofa.

I turned back toward the kitchen. My intention was to watch TV for a bit, but since he was there, I figured I would hang out in the kitchen instead. If he occupied a room, I would rather go to a different room. The less I was around him, the better off I'd be.

Mom came out of her bedroom and walked into the kitchen to greet me. She gave me a hug and asked me how my day went.

"Fine," I said as I grabbed the cookies out of the cupboard. I was always hungry when I came home from school. I poured myself a glass of milk as mom opened the cookies.

"Did you end up getting a hold of Jake last night?" she asked as she took cookies out of the package and set them on the counter.

"No, but I saw him in school today," I replied as I walked over to the table and sat down. Mom followed me with the stack of cookies and sat down.

"Is this someone I should know about?" mom asked as she leaned over the table and peered into my eyes.

It made me feel uncomfortable, so I quickly looked away. "Just a friend?" mom asked inquisitively.

I nodded as I busied myself with dipping my cookie in the milk. "Are you sure about that?" she asked with a smirk on her face.

"Yes, mom, He's just a friend." I tried to look convincing, but she saw right through it.

The phone rang just then. She picked it up and answered. I was really glad for the distraction. Anything to get out of this conversation with mom. The last thing I wanted to talk to her about was boys.

Mom handed the phone to me. "It's Tricia," she said.

Just who I wanted to talk to. I wanted to talk to her about Jake and Tim. The problem was that mom was right there. I needed to talk to her in private, so I asked her if she could come over for a while. She ended up coming after supper. It seemed like forever before she got there! I couldn't wait to tell her about Jake and Tim. We went straight to my room, and I told her about Jake asking us to go to the movies. She was ecstatic about the news.

"Yes! Yes!" she exclaimed as she jumped in victory. I asked, "Think your mom will let you go?"

Tricia instantly went still. "No Way."

"Mine neither. How can we go without them knowing?" I asked.

Tricia's face lit up with an idea, "How about if you act like you are staying at my house, and I act like I am staying at your house? Think that will work?"

I thought about it for a minute and smiled big at her. Yeah! Then I had a thought. "Wait, where can they pick us up?"

"We could walk," replied Tricia.

"It's on the other side of town," I interjected.

"I know, but that's all I could think of," replied Tricia.

The next day at school, our problems were solved. We both got an invitation to Ginger's birthday party. It was a sleepover Friday night! At lunch, we talked about it and decided it was the best way to do this.

As long as we went to an early show, we could go to Ginger's afterward, and nobody would ever know the difference. The only problem is who would drive us, but we could figure that out later. We asked our parents if we could go and they both said yes. I told

Jake we could only go to the first movie, and then we would have to leave for Ginger's birthday bash. He was fine with that.

I thought about it for a minute, and then a light bulb came on. I asked him if his brother would be able to pick us up after school and we could just hang out somewhere until we go to the movies. I didn't want him to know that our parents had no clue what our plans were. This would be one way to get around our moms. I was hoping he didn't read into what we were doing.

Jake shrugged his shoulders and said, "I'm sure he would. Why not?"

We were so excited! We both couldn't wait until Friday. We told our parents Ginger wanted us to come home with her on the bus. Thursday, mom wrote a note for me to ride the bus to Ginger's house. I felt so guilty while she wrote it. I hated all of this lying. It made me feel so bad. Arrangements were made, and we were free to go.

After school, Jake's brother picked up the four of us and dropped us off at the video game place in town. We hung out there for a while.

Jake and I were flirting back and forth, and suddenly, he wrapped his arms around me and gave me a great big kiss right on the lips! My heart fluttered and I had butterflies in my stomach. He took me by surprise, leaving me speechless. All I could do was stare at him with this stupid look on my face.

He leaned closer to my ear and whispered, "I really like you, Samantha."

I sputtered out how I liked him, too. It came out high-pitched and screechy because I couldn't catch my breath. I was swept away in my emotions, as I had never been kissed by a boy before. It was all so new to me.

That evening at the movies, Jake and I sat in the front seat with his older brother. Jake put his arm around me and I snuggled into him. It felt so good to be so close to him. It was the best time I ever had. I never knew it could feel so good when someone you really liked showed you so much attention.

A quick thought went through my head about mom. No wonder she liked having Carl around so much. She must love the attention he gives her. I guess I couldn't blame her. My thoughts were broken when Jake pulled me closer and kissed my cheek. I felt butterflies again as his lips touched my cheek.

Tim and Tricia got along so well together. They were both loud and laughing throughout the whole movie. The next thing you know, all was quiet in the back seat. I turned around to look, and Tim had his arm around Tricia. She looked at me with shining eyes and smiled big. I knew right then she was really liking Tim. She winked at me, and I smiled back at her.

When the movie was over, I realized we didn't have a ride to Ginger's house. How stupid of us! We thought of everything but the ride to the party.

Tricia reluctantly asked Jake's brother if he could take us to Ginger's house. He acted like it was no problem.

The next movie started. I looked back at Tricia in alarm. He planned on waiting until the next movie was over before he took us to Ginger's! I started to panic. It would be way too late to show up for her party if we didn't leave until after the movie. We were already pushing it just by leaving now.

Finally, Tricia leaned toward the front seat and asked, "I hate to do this to you, but could you take us now?"

"What? Well, sure, I guess," he said as he started the car. We both apologized all the way to Ginger's house for ruining their movie night. They all kept saying it was okay, but we both felt so stupid.

As we pulled into Ginger's driveway, my heart sank. A vehicle that looked just like mom's was sitting in the driveway. I shook it off, thinking I was just being paranoid. It couldn't be. Then, suddenly, right in front of my eyes was Tricia's mom! I looked back at Tricia with wide, fearful eyes. We were in huge trouble.

Mom opened the door of her car and came running out as Jake's brother put his car in park. Jake started to say something as he went to reach for me. I dodged him and lunged for the door. I jumped right over him and out of the car before mom got to me. Tricia was out of the car just as fast as I was.

"I had fun, see you Monday!" I quickly said and closed the door. Just then, mom grabbed a hold of me by the shirt. Tricia was already in her mom's grip. They pretty much dragged us to the vehicles right in front of Jake and Tim. I looked back in hopes that they weren't seeing this, but there they were, wide-eyed and mouths gaping. How embarrassing.

Mom was screaming at me but I didn't hear a word she said. All I could think of was how would I ever explain this to Jake? Would he even still like me? My heart was racing and my head began to hurt.

Mom yelled at me all the way home, but all I could think of was Jake. Will he ever talk to me again? I knew I wouldn't find out until Monday. There was no way I would have any phone privileges after this. As for that goes, I probably won't have any privileges at all for a long time. Suddenly, I missed dad.

Chapter Fourteen

My Birthday

At last, I could get out of here and go to dad's. I came home from school and packed up. I couldn't wait to leave. The past week has been a nightmare. Mom hardly talked to me (not that I really cared), and I couldn't go anywhere or do anything. She took the TV and radio out of my room and everything. I have never seen her so mad at me. It just seems to get worse and worse.

Going to school every day was a relief. I was never so thankful for school in my life! At least I got to see Tricia and Jake there. Jake still talked to me, by the way. I was grateful for that much. He asked me what happened, so I had no way out of it. I had to tell him the truth.

I was so afraid he would never talk to me again, but he just smiled at me and said, "Cool."

I smiled at him and said, "Cool, now I can't do anything. She grounded me and took away my TV and everything."

Jake shrugged, "She'll get over it. It won't last forever." I rolled my eyes as I said, "You don't know my mom."

He laughed and said, "Let me know when I can call you again." "Probably never," I muttered.

Jake and I met in between each class. I loved him waiting for me at my locker. He would walk me to each of my classes. That made me feel so important. It was so cool to have all of his attention aimed at little ole me.

Tricia and I got to talk at lunch every day and also on the bus ride home. She was in just as much trouble as I was, but she at least got to keep her TV and music in her room. Lucky! At least she can pass the time watching TV or listening to music.

I just wish I would have told mom the truth and asked to go to the movies. She probably wouldn't have let me go, but at least I wouldn't be in this much trouble.

A horn went off, and I snapped out of my deep thoughts over the past week. Dad was here to pick me up. I grabbed my stuff and ran out the door. I couldn't get out of there fast enough. Mom hollered bye to me and I just ignored it. Good riddance, I thought as I ran to dad's truck. Hope to not see you again for a long time.

Once I got to dad's, I found out it wasn't going to be much better. He lectured me about what I did all the way to his house. Even Lindy was acting funny toward me. I didn't get it. Why was everyone acting like they hated me? It felt like everyone liked me according to how good I was. I didn't know my parents could do such a thing. They couldn't have been more obvious if they stood there with their arms crossed and their backs to me. I wanted to yell, "Get over it already! Stop treating me like this!"

My birthday was coming up next week, and I thought we would be celebrating it at dad's, but he said no, not after what I pulled. I went into my room and lay across my bed. It made me wonder if I would have a birthday at all this year.

Dad had me working all weekend. He said it was my punishment for sneaking off with a boy. I never thought he would be this mad about it. I spent my whole weekend pulling weeds, cleaning the house, and helping dad clean his garage. It really kind of sucked, but at least he let me watch TV in the evenings.

Saturday afternoon, everything kind of caught up to me. I thought about how mom was acting all week and now how dad and Lindy were acting. Then I thought about my birthday and how everyone seemed to be passing it by like it was nothing important. It all hit me at once and I sat on my bed and just cried. I really cried hard. I was tired of how everyone was treating me. I felt neglected and alone. I felt like nobody liked me at all.

Lindy popped her head in the door after a few minutes. "You okay?" She asked with concern in her voice. There was a long pause. "You want me to go get your dad?" she asked.

"No, it's okay," I said. Then I started to sob. Lindy came in and sat next to me. She gave me a hug and told me that everything would be okay and would work out in the end. Once I calmed down a bit, she left the room. The next thing I knew dad was coming in. She must have gone out and told him about me breaking down. I talked to dad a little, and things seemed better after that.

The next day, Lindy made me a birthday cake. I felt so much better knowing I was at least going to have a birthday party.

I went with Lindy to the store to pick out the ice cream and a few decorations. Dad came in, and I showed him what we bought. He seemed really happy about our decorations. It felt good to feel like things were normal again.

While Lindy and I put up the decorations, I thanked her for the cake and for everything she was doing for me. I told her I didn't think I was going to have a birthday at all.

She stopped for a second and looked at me seriously and said, "You know, what made your dad so mad is that you were with a boy."

"But I didn't do anything. There were five of us together. We weren't even alone," I said, exasperated.

Lindy looked at me and raised one eyebrow.

"I mean it, we didn't do anything. I'm really being honest, Lindy," I said, trying to convince her.

"Good, it's so good to hear that," said Lindy as she turned her attention back to the ribbon she was hanging.

"Not to lecture you or anything, but your mom and dad are just looking out for you. They are trying to protect you, and don't want you to end up in a bad situation. They want what is best for you," said Lindy.

I decided to let my guard down with Lindy. She kind of reminded me of a friend the way she was acting toward me.

I told her, "I know, but I really had a lot of fun, and I really like Jake a lot. I just wish they would let me do more."

Lindy decided to tell it as it was. She said, "Well, I know you might not believe it now, but what you did could have led to real trouble. Sometimes, the choices we make end up affecting us for the rest of our lives."

"Yeah, I know," I said as I thought about how much I appreciated her talking to me about this stuff. I really needed someone to talk to because mom and dad certainly wouldn't talk to me. They would just get mad at me.

I had my birthday party that evening at dad's. Grandma and Grandpa came over. My Aunt also came with a few of my cousins. It was a blast!

They all sang to me as my face turned bright red. They giggled about it, and so did I. My birthday wish was to see Jake more often. I blew out all the candles in one try.

Grandma and Grandpa gave me a beautiful butterfly necklace. My cousins gave me some makeup and a few body lotions. Dad and Lindy gave me a huge keyboard on a stand. I couldn't wait to set it up in my new room. I always wanted a keyboard, but never expected one so huge.

Lindy told me she played the piano in her younger years, and she promised to teach me how to play. I was really excited to learn. Dad set it up and Lindy showed me a few things on it.

It wasn't long before it was time to go back to mom's house. We were running about an hour late, and mom still didn't greet me at the door. Go figure.

"Sam, is that you?" Mom called from the kitchen.

"Yeah, it's me," I said as I took off my shoes and walked in to join her. She was in the middle of cooking supper. I sat down in dad's kitchen chair.

Mom looked at me and smiled. "I was just thinking about calling your dad," she said as she glanced at the clock.

"We had my birthday party, so we were running late," I replied. "Oh, did you eat supper?" she asked.

"Yeah, we ate before we had cake and ice cream," I said.

"Okay, do me a favor, sweety and set the table," she said as she cooked away.

I stood up and went to the cupboard. I turned toward mom and asked, "How many?"

"For four, unless you want something," mom said as she stirred the food on the stovetop.

I was disappointed to find out that Carl and the boys would be eating here. He must be on his way because the Lord knows you would hear the boys if they were here.

"How come you didn't tell me about your bedroom set?" mom asked.

"Well, with the news of you and Carl and all that happened in the past few weeks, I just didn't find the right time to tell you." I rolled my eyes, thinking I tried to tell you, but you were too busy with Carl.

She nodded her head in agreement but looked at me regretfully. She walked over to me and put her arm around my shoulder. She recounted as she spoke, "You know, there has been an awful lot going on around here lately. What do you say we calm things down a little bit and go for a little walk after supper? Just you and I?"

"Sounds good," I said in joy. We used to go for walks all the time until Carl came around. I really missed doing little things like that with mom.

Besides, I think we needed to talk a little and reconnect ourselves. There was so much tension between us. I thought about how sorry I was for sneaking off and making such a mess of things.

Then, the ruckus began. In came Carl and the boys. I looked at mom and rolled my eyes. Mom whispered to be nice. I walked into the entryway and greeted them all, being as friendly as I could. I quickly excused myself and went to my room. Carl seemed really disappointed that I wasn't sitting down with them to eat.

Mom came into my room to get me after dinner was over. "Are you ready?" she asked all peppy.

"Yep," I said as I set my book down on the bed.

"What are you reading?" she asked as she went over and picked my book up.

"Oh, it's just a book…" I replied. I really didn't want her to see it. I picked it up at the school library.

"Well, of course, Sam…" she trailed off as she read the title. She just stood there for a minute, not knowing what to say.

"Mom, it's just a book," I pleaded.

"I know, let's go," she said as she decided to dismiss the subject.

As we walked, she asked me about the book again. I hesitated to tell her about it. She encouraged me that she could take it and to just tell her about it.

"Okay, It's about a girl whose parents are divorced, and she sounds a lot like me and, I mean, her life... And I just thought it would be interesting to see how it goes for her." I looked over at mom as we walked. I could see the sadness in her eyes. I felt bad for even reading it, let alone telling her about it. It's not like I meant to hurt her, but I felt guilty.

"Mom," I said regretfully, "I didn't mean to make you sad."

"It's okay, sweetheart. You read it and maybe it'll even help you out some," she said in an uneven tone.

"Yeah, maybe it will help me to understand things a little better..." I trailed off in deep thought.

"So tell me about your bedroom outfit." mom said, changing the subject.

I perked up. I haven't even had time to be excited about it with everything happening so fast and all. I told her how beautiful it was. I told her about the canopy bed and the light pink flowers on the dressers. I told her about the wall decals Lindy got me. I told her about the trinket box Lindy got me before we even picked out a bedroom outfit and how it matched perfectly. I even told her about the bed doll we made together and how beautiful it was on the bed.

"It looks so pretty just sitting there, Mom. You should see it. Maybe you can come over sometime and see it for yourself the next time I go to dad's," I said with excitement.

"Sounds like Lindy and you are patching things up," she said in a small voice.

I stopped and thought about it. I talked more about Lindy and me than I did dad. I guess I didn't realize until now that I am making more memories with her than with my own dad. What happened?

I replied at last, "Yeah, she's really nice to me now. She's actually pretty cool."

"I am so glad to hear that. It makes me feel better about you going over there," She said.

"Yeah, I don't mind her at all," I spurted out as I thought of Carl and how I avoided him.

Maybe I should give him a chance. It would make mom happier anyway.

"So, I kind of want to talk a little about boys..." she trailed off.

Oh no, here goes…

"What is really going on with you and this Jake kid?" she asked.

"Well, I like him a lot. He's really nice. He isn't a bad kid, mom, I promise," I begged her to believe me.

She put her hands palms up and asked, "Why on earth did you sneak out with him?"

"Because he invited us, and we knew you guys wouldn't let us go.

He had no clue what we were doing. He didn't have anything to do with it, mom. He didn't even know our plans to sneak away. I promise he wasn't involved in it at all," I said, trying to convince her. I just wanted her to believe me.

"I'm sure he knows now," mom muttered.

"Yeah, I had to tell him. I didn't have a choice," I recalled.

Mom went on to tell me I was not allowed to go to the movies with boys. She said I was way too young.

"Mom," I pleaded, "We all went together, and nobody went off alone. We didn't do anything but watch a movie."

"Who was driving?" she asked.

"Jake's older brother. He stayed with us the whole time," I replied.

"What should we do about your birthday? I mean, what do you propose we do when you are grounded and all?" mom asked.

I shrugged my shoulders.

"Maybe we should just have it with the two of us," she suggested.

I begged her to let me at least have Tricia and Jake over. She said maybe Tricia, and I pleaded to let Jake come too. I reminded her that he didn't do anything wrong.

"Well, I guess I could meet him this way," she said as she gave in.

"Yes! You will like him, mom. He is so nice and such a great person!" I said with excitement.

Mom stopped walking for a minute and said, "But just for a few hours, and that's it. I want to meet this Jake and see what he is like for myself."

"Oh, you will like him, mom. You will. Just wait and see. He's so cute!" I exclaimed, all excited about them coming to my birthday party.

I reached over and gave mom a big hug. I was so glad she wasn't going to keep me away from my friends on my birthday. I wanted her to meet Jake so she could see for herself that he really was a very nice person.

Mom smiled and began her lecture mode. She lectured me about how girls can get themselves into bad situations without even realizing it until it's too late. She told me how dangerous it could be to sneak off without anyone knowing where you are. She talked about peer pressure and how it can make you do things you don't want to do. I didn't think she would ever stop!

As she continued to talk, I began to realize how bad of a decision we made by sneaking off. She was right. I apologized to her several times and promised I would never do it again.

Wednesday came along, and I was so excited! It was my birthday, and Tricia brought me some birthday balloons to school. That was awesome! The whole day, I felt like I was on top of the world. When I got home, mom greeted me with a big happy birthday hug and kiss.

"I have a surprise for you," she said with excitement in her voice. "What is it?" I asked as I smiled at her.

"Oh, something I think you will really like," she said with a great big, sly-looking grin on her face.

"Come on, mom, tell me!" I said as I put my hands together and begged.

She laughed and said, "Okay, come with me."

We walked over to the back door as she told me my surprise was from her and Carl. She had me close my eyes. She walked me out onto the back patio and told me to open my eyes. I froze for a second, soaking up what I was seeing. I ran down the stairs and suddenly stopped dead in my tracks and stared disbelievingly at my gift.

I was so excited! There stood Carl with the bicycle I'd been wanting for so long!

I have been bugging mom to let me get a bike to ride to school forever. My very own bike! The very one I asked for over and over again! I ran over to the bike and looked at every detail. Mom came walking out.

"Mom, I love it!" I said. "Take it for a spin," she said.

I jumped on it and rode it to the front of the house and down the driveway. It was perfect. I came back to mom and Carl and gave them both a hug, telling them how thankful I was. They were both smiling and laughing as they saw how excited I was.

I rode it back and forth down the road until everyone showed up for my birthday party.

Carl disappeared for a while and when he returned, he had Taylor and Bradley. I was disappointed for a minute, but then I decided I wasn't going to let them ruin my day. I just hoped they wouldn't act like idiots and embarrass me in front of Tricia and Jake.

Before long, Tricia and Jake were there. My grandma came too. My Aunt unexpectedly came with my two cousins. I don't know how happy mom was since I was supposed to only have Tricia and Jake there, but I was so glad to see them.

Carl cooked hot dogs and hamburgers on the grill, and mom brought out the macaroni salad she made earlier. Grandma brought a salad and some homemade macaroni and cheese. The food was all so good! We ate supper and went straight to the cake and ice cream. Everyone was pretty full by the time we were done. I opened my presents, and it was all over before I knew it.

We all had a great time messing around in the yard. We took turns riding on my bike and played volleyball. I was glad my cousins came so they could meet Jake, too. It turned out to be a great birthday, and I was very surprised that Taylor and Bradley acted fine.

We all sat in the living room to rest after everyone left. I sat in the middle of the floor, going through all my gifts. Taylor and Bradley sat down beside me looking through everything with me.

Carl finally stood up and told the boys it was time to go. They told me happy birthday and said goodbye. I guess they weren't as bad as I thought they were. In fact, I was beginning to like them.

My favorite present was the heart shaped necklace Jake got me. I adored it! I put it on and mom complimented what a pretty necklace it was. She knew it was from Jake and gave me a big wink. I smiled, all puffed up from all the attention I received all day. It was great to be the star of the party. Finally, it was all about me.

I asked mom if she liked Jake. She told me he seemed like a respectful young man. I smiled at her and agreed.

By nighttime, mom reminded me that I would still be grounded for another week. Oh well, back to real life. I didn't want to think about that. I just wanted to think about what a great day I had. She told me good night, and I fell right to sleep.

Chapter Fifteen

Moving???

On Saturday morning, I woke up and immediately thought of being grounded. That meant no fun at all today. At least I could go to school and see my friends on weekdays. I thought about how boring it would be just sitting around the house all day with no TV, music or anything. Yuck! I played with the idea of staying in bed for a while, but the aroma of eggs and bacon came seeping through my bedroom door.

A smile came across my face as I got out of bed. Mom was cooking breakfast. I looked forward to spending my Saturday morning with mom. I got dressed and stopped to take a good whiff of the breakfast smell. Boy, did it smell good!

I walked toward the kitchen, anxious to help mom with breakfast. I loved spending our mornings together like this. It didn't happen very often since I go to dad's a lot. It was a special treat to spend time with mom.

As I walked through the living room, I stopped and looked over at the TV. I wondered why it was on, then grabbed the remote and shut it off. Mom never watched TV in the morning. She always listened to the radio instead. I shook it off and set the remote down.

I heard low voices coming from the kitchen. My heart sank as I thought of Carl. I didn't want him to be here. I wanted it to just be mom and I. It just spoiled the whole morning, knowing someone was here. I heard some giggling and realized it was probably Martha. Those two were always giggling and acting silly when they were together. Regardless of who was here, I knew my special morning with mom was ruined. Even though I didn't like Martha, I secretly hoped it was her. It would be better than Carl, anyway.

"Samantha, is that you?" mom called out. "Yeah," I mumbled.

"I was just about to come get you. Breakfast is ready" she said.

I went into the kitchen, and low and behold, there was Carl. To my surprise, the boys were here too. They were sitting at the table, goofing around like usual. That must have been where the giggling came in.

Mom stood at the stove, taking eggs out of the pan, while Carl stood behind her with his arms wrapped around her waist. He kissed her on her neck and whispered in her ear. She started giggling. I hated how close he was to her. It made me want to throw up. All I could think of was go home, Carl, go home and take your boys with you. I wanted to say it out loud but knew it would land me in my room with no breakfast.

"Good morning, mom," I said as I stood at the table, not knowing where to sit.

Mom and Carl both turned their heads, and Carl backed away from mom. Just what I wished for.

Mom smiled at me and said, "Good morning, sweety."

I decided now was a good time to let Carl know he wasn't the only special one in the house. I went up to mom and gave her a great big hug. She was taken aback by it at first, but then she gave me a big bear hug. It felt good, but I was too busy looking over at Carl to see if he was jealous. I was disappointed to see that there was no reaction at all from him. I helped mom take the food to the table, hoping he would feel left out. Instead, he went to the fridge and poured us all a glass of orange juice.

As I took the food to the table, Carl put the orange juice on the table and sat down right where dad used to sit. I couldn't handle it. I walked over to him and stood there, not knowing what to say. I was screaming inside! He could never replace my dad!

I finally got the nerve to speak. I knew I had to be careful what I said, or mom would be mad at me. I didn't want to ruin breakfast.

"Can I sit there?" I asked cautiously.

Carl raised his brow in confusion. I think he heard the tension in my voice. Mom froze right where she was. She looked very irritated.

"Sure," Carl shrugged and moved to the next chair.

I decided to explain it to him. I wanted him to feel uncomfortable. I hoped it would make him feel out of place, like he didn't belong here, and go home where he belonged.

"This was my dad's chair, you know, when mom and dad were together. It just wouldn't be right for you to sit in his chair," I said with a slight attitude.

"Samantha!" mom yelled. Everyone went quiet.

"I see," Carl said with defeat as he fidgeted in his chair. It worked!

He felt uncomfortable. Just my plan. Now, if he would just take his boys and go home.

I plopped in dad's chair triumphantly.

I was about to continue rubbing it in when mom popped up right next to me with the plate of toast. She leaned over really close to me as she placed the plate on the table. She was right in my face.

"But your father isn't anywhere near here, now, is he?" she said with venom in her voice. She glared at me, with her eyes piercing right to the core of my being. Her look told me definitely not to push it, so I cleared my throat and politely asked to pass the eggs.

Breakfast tasted delicious, but the company was horrible. I just kept to myself as mom and Carl chatted away. The boys were talking amongst themselves. I just sat there listening to the conversation. I really felt angry because now I was the one that felt out of place. Irony…it sucked!

Carl and mom stopped talking, and they both looked at me. They exchanged glances and returned their attention to me. I knew something was up. I was concerned about what was coming this time. They seem to never cease to amaze and confuse me.

"You want to tell her?" Mom asked Carl. "You probably should," said Carl.

Mom started talking. She told me how they were thinking about taking things one step further in their relationship.

My heart sank. They were already planning to get married. What else can they surprise me with? I knew things were never going to be the same again. Not like they were, anyway.

"We have decided we want to live together," mom spoke in anticipation.

I was so surprised. I didn't expect it to be like this. I thought maybe they were going to wait until they were married. Mom's divorce wasn't even final yet. I expected this to be at least a year down the road.

I looked around the table, noticing that everyone was silent, even the boys. They were all waiting for my reaction. I knew they all thought I was going to blow up and act like a fool, but I wanted to prove them all wrong. I just sat there silently.

Carl spoke up, "Your mom and I love each other very much and want to be together all the time."

I couldn't believe my ears. I was completely stunned. I could feel myself losing control. I wanted to scream at him. I wanted to tell him to shut up.

Suddenly, my stomach started doing flip-flops.

Mom said, "We are going to move into Carl's house. Since this house isn't big enough for all of us."

I panicked! I tried to convince her our house is plenty big enough. I knew that it wasn't, but I didn't care. I just wanted to stay here. My stomach was feeling really upset, and my head started whirling.

Carl reminded me that he has two boys and told me there wasn't room for three more people here. He told me he had two extra rooms in his house. He suggested remodeling one and making it just the way I wanted.

I just shook my head. I couldn't understand all of this nonsense. It just couldn't be happening. Why won't they just wait until they get married? No way was I going to move. This is where I was supposed to grow up.

I suddenly felt really sick. I ran to the bathroom and leaned over the toilet. I made it just in time to throw up all of my breakfast.

Mom came into the bathroom and asked if I was okay. I was still leaning over the toilet, waiting for my stomach to settle. She grabbed a Kleenex and handed it to me as she rubbed my back. I started to feel a little better and sat on the floor in front of the toilet. I had no strength left in me to even get up.

"I know it's a big change, hunny. We can adapt together," she said as she sat on the edge of the tub.

I looked up at her and pleaded with my eyes. I begged, "I don't want to move, mom."

"I know, neither do I, but this house just isn't big enough for all of us," she stated as a matter of factly.

"Can't we just add on like dad did?" I asked, hoping it might plant a seed.

No, that is way too expensive. Besides, Carl has a beautiful home that is plenty big enough for all of us. You saw it, you know how beautiful it is." she said, almost looking guilty.

Just then, I knew why we went to his house that day to meet the boys. They planned this all along. She was hoping I would want to live there. I recounted how she mentioned to me how nice it would be to live in a home like this.

"What about school?" I asked as I thought about my friends, especially Tricia and Jake.

"Well, you can finish the year out here and switch schools next year. We won't be moving for a little while anyway." She tried to sound encouraging.

"I don't want to go to a new school, mom. I can't do it, mom, please…" I pleaded with her as tears started streaming down my cheeks.

"Hunny, we will both have a lot of adjusting to do. Don't worry, Carl's boys will introduce you to some kids your age. You will meet plenty of people during the summer. That way, you will know at least a few people when school starts. You have lots of time before you have to switch."

I knew there was no talking her into anything. Her mind was made up, and that was that. My future was ruined. Ever since Carl came into our lives, things just seem to get worse and worse. I felt like I couldn't get any lower than this. I was definitely at the bottom. Nothing could get worse than this. New school, new house, new families on both sides…the list goes on. It was definitely the worst it could get.

I went to my room and spent the next few hours there. I didn't care if I ever came out of my room again. At least I didn't have to see Carl, then. I despised him for meeting mom. I resented him for taking away my whole life. If they wanted to ruin my life, they were doing a very good job. I just couldn't believe all of this. I even despised mom for doing this to me.

Mom popped into my room after about two hours and asked me if I wanted to go to Carl's to pick out my room. I just shook my head. I didn't even look at her. I couldn't look at her even if I tried. I felt like she betrayed me.

I wondered when we were going to move, but I didn't want to talk to either of them. I was sitting there just dying to know when. I just couldn't talk to them to find out. I felt if I spoke one word I would just burst out in tears. I was speechless.

I felt so alone just sitting there on my bed, looking around at things in my room. This was my room, but for how long? This room was my life. This is where mom and dad tucked me in at night over the years. This was where mom would read me bedtime stories. This was the house I grew up in.

All the memories were kicking in. I couldn't just let it all go so easily. How could mom do this to me? I couldn't make sense out of any of this mess. I suddenly had a huge desire to talk to Jake. I just had to call him, but I was grounded. I couldn't talk to him or to anybody else. I was completely alone. I put my hands over my face and cried.

Mom eventually came into my room to talk to me. She basically said her feelings were strong for Carl. She tried to explain how they planned to wait to move in together, but they couldn't stand to be away from each other.

"But what about me, mom? Where do I fit in?" I asked, pleading with her.

"Hunny, this isn't about you. I know you don't want to move, but things change in life. You have to give it some time to get used to it. That's why we are telling you now. We won't be moving for a few months," she said as she tried to encourage me.

She didn't understand how much she was ruining my whole life. Thinking of moving to a new school made me sick to my stomach. It seemed way too scary to just up and change my whole life like that. I wished I could just disappear.

I sat and tried to listen to her, but I couldn't stop thinking about walking through a school by myself, not knowing anybody. The thought was horrifying. I wish Carl would leave forever and we could stay where we were.

Thinking of Carl put a spike of hatred in my heart. I liked my life like it was before Carl came into the picture. He came in and ruined everything. I resented him for taking away everything I loved, including mom.

The rest of the weekend seemed to last forever. It slowly passed as I watched the second hand ticking away. What a drag it was to sit in my room by myself most of the time. I couldn't watch TV or listen to music. All I could do was read and think.

It really stunk that I couldn't talk to Tricia or Jake. I thought about how much I would miss them and wondered if I would ever see them again after I moved. I cried at the thought of losing all that I had here. My friends, my teachers, my school, my house, my room and even my mom. It was too overwhelming.

I stood up and looked at myself in the mirror. My eyes were puffy and red from crying so much. I looked like a mess! I had to get myself together so I could go to school tomorrow, I thought. I can't go to school looking like this. I looked like the Walking Dead. I grabbed my makeup and started putting it on, hoping it would take some of the puffiness down and I could at least make myself look halfway decent.

As I finished with the makeup, mom came into my room for the hundredth time that day.

She sat on my bed and said, "I see you are feeling a little better." I shrugged my shoulders and put away my mascara.

"Anyway, we are going to Carl's for supper. I thought we could do something afterward," said mom.

I just nodded my head. I wasn't going to give her the satisfaction of seeing me upset anymore. She had done that enough lately. After the news I've been given, nothing can affect me now.

I leaned in real close to the mirror. The makeup seemed to work a little. I hoped I would look better tomorrow. After all, I didn't want Jake to see me like this.

Monday came as a relief to me. I woke up early and got ready for school. It was so exciting to get away from all the stress at home and see my friends. It would be nice to feel normal again.

I rode my bike to school that morning. It was the first day of not being grounded. I felt free for a change! I went to school so early the doors were still locked when I got there. I waited patiently, anxious to see Tricia and Jake soon. I sat on the curb, thinking of all the things that had happened in the last few weeks. What a mess!

A few cars pulled up and dropped off some kids. Before I knew it, a group of kids surrounded me. It was comforting to be around familiar faces, yet it was sad knowing this would all soon be over.

The doors opened and off we all went down the halls. I heard the familiar chatting as lockers slammed shut and laughter filled the halls. I quietly stood at my locker, looking around at the commotion and flood of students. I grew so fond of this school. This was my comfort zone. Sadness filled me as I thought of how this would all come to an end very soon.

"Samantha! I missed you so much!" Tricia cried out as she grabbed me from behind. She gave me a bear hug, holding tight around my arms. I tried to break free as she giggled. I turned around with a big smile on my face as she let go.

"Hi," I said, trying so hard to be cheery.

Her smile left as soon as she saw my face. Oops, I guess makeup didn't work.

"Hey, what's wrong?" she asked with concern in her voice.

Tricia was definitely my best friend. She even saw through my fake smile. She truly knew me well.

"Nothing, I…uh…I gotta go," I whispered as I tried not to get choked up.

I closed my locker and went directly to class. I couldn't talk to her yet. It would just make me cry and look like an idiot in front of the whole school. I didn't want to make a scene.

Jake even noticed something was wrong. He passed me a note in class asking me what the deal was. I didn't want to get all emotional, so I just shrugged my shoulders and didn't answer his note. He asked me again between classes, but I didn't really want to talk about it. How could I get it together enough to tell them?

By lunch time I finally had a chance to tell Tricia about moving. She was shocked. She couldn't believe I would be going to another school. By the time lunch was over, we were both teary-eyed. I let out a sigh as I paused at my classroom door. This was so hard to comprehend.

At the end of the day, Jake came running up to me. "Sam, Tricia told me you were moving. Is that true?" he asked.

I took a deep breath and tried to speak. Nothing came out but a squeak. I nodded my head silently for fear I would cry if I tried to say anything.

"When? Where?" he asked urgently. He was obviously upset.

I really started to cry then. He grabbed me, rubbing the back of my head as he held me tight. It felt so good. It gave me chills up and down my spine to be so close to him.

Butterflies were swirling in my stomach, and my heart was breaking at the same time. My emotions were going crazy! I didn't know you could feel so many feelings all at one time. I felt lonely, comforted, loved, torn, happy, unfortunate and lucky all at once.

I sobbed as he held me in his arms. He was so loving, so tender. I would miss him even more than Tricia. Then and there, I knew he was the one for me. I truly loved him! My heart broke even more as I came to realize he was the one I wanted to marry someday.

By the middle of the week, Tricia and I were trying to figure out how I could stay in this school. We went through so many possibilities but couldn't come up with anything practical enough.

Thursday afternoon, Tricia, Tim, Jake, and I all met at my house and rode our bikes to the park. We put our brains together and tried to figure out how I could stay in this school. Jake came up with a great idea. I could talk to my dad and see if I could live with him. He lived in another town, but he lived close enough that maybe Lindy would drive me back and forth to school. She didn't work anyway, so she could do that. We planned things out for our benefit, thinking dad and Lindy wouldn't mind.

Boy, was I wrong!

Chapter Sixteen

Counting on Friends

Dad came to get me on Friday afternoon. I couldn't wait to ask if I could live with him and have Lindy take me back and forth to school each day. When he came to get me, I told him about our plan. That was a big mistake. He actually stopped the truck on the side of the road and chewed me out for expecting so much out of Lindy. He was really angry. I was surprised at his reaction. I didn't understand why he got so mad, but he was just yelling at me. I don't remember seeing him like this before.

Finally, he stopped yelling and just sat there for a few minutes. He calmed down for a bit and started to drive again. It was a quiet ride to his house, that was for sure. I was afraid to say anything because I didn't want to make him mad again.

When we pulled into the driveway, dad told me to come into the garage for a minute. I followed him, hoping he wasn't going to yell anymore. He stood in the garage, just looking at me for a while. It felt like he was burning holes through me. It seemed like an eternity before he spoke.

He said," Your mother and I are plain sick and tired of your attitude. You need to figure out how to adjust to whatever life gives you. Everything in life does not have to revolve around what you want."

I had my head down as I stared at my feet. I nervously glanced up at him as my head stayed lowered. My eyes darted back and forth, not knowing what to do. I was defeated for sure. I felt like a dog with its tail between its legs.

He continued, "You gave Lindy a hard time for quite a while. I know you are doing better now, but you were very rude to her, and I let it go. Now you've moved on to the next person, and I am tired of you acting like a spoiled rotten brat. You've been giving your mother a hard time ever since she met this guy, and you haven't even given him a chance. You antagonize and act rude to him for no reason at all, just like you did to Lindy. Now, suddenly you want to move in and Have Lindy be at your beck and call? I don't think so!"

Apparently mom told him everything that was going on with Carl.

I stared hard at my feet by then, trying to concentrate on the grooves in my shoes. I tried to tune him out, but it wasn't happening. I felt horrible thinking that dad didn't even understand. He really hurt my feelings, but that wasn't the worst part.

The thought of never seeing Jake and Tricia again was my worst problem. It all settled around them. I loved them and nobody even had a clue how I was feeling.

He chewed me out for quite a while and then asked me if I was okay. Sure, I was okay, other than the fact that my whole life would change in a short time. Other than the fact that I will be losing my very best friend in the whole world. Besides the fact that I will never see Jake ever again. Yes, I was just fine. And what did I say to dad? Yep, and that's all. Just a simple little Yep.

It was finished. My relationship with mom and dad both became an emotionless, cold pit from that point forward. They were both against me, and I was determined that they wouldn't hurt me anymore. I was angry at both of them. I was mad because they were so ignorant to put me in this divorced mess when I didn't even ask for it. I was mad because I didn't know where I fit in with all of this mess. In fact, I wanted them together, not divorced. I was angry because they always thought of themselves without any regard for me, and yet they thought I was the selfish one. They couldn't see things from my point of view even for a second. They only knew what they wanted and closed out any thoughts or feelings I had.

It was just over. I was done with all of this. No more whiny little girl. No more heartfelt tears. Life was not going to beat me up anymore. I was done feeling lost and confused.

Right then and there, I decided I was no longer going to depend on mom and dad to make me happy. I would make myself happy no matter what the situation was.

The change was instantly obvious. Dad even peered into my eyes and asked me why I was looking so strange. The sweet little Samantha, who was always wearing her heart on her sleeve, was gone. The new persona took over, and I knew life would be better. No more tears. No more begging and pleading for anything. From now on, I will find my own way through life's struggles.

I closed myself in my room for quite some time after dad chewed me out. I was in deep thought. What did I want in life? What would make me happy? I thought long and hard about it. There was only one answer to all of this insanity…Jake. That was what I really wanted.

I suddenly didn't care about dad's attention or even mom's affection. I just wanted to be with Jake. I loved him and needed him in my life. mom and dad were always talking about needing someone in their lives. Well, I needed Jake in my life. Yes, I needed someone just like they did. They were so concerned with their own affairs that it felt like I didn't fit anywhere. It's like they just plain forgot about me. Well, now I have Jake to turn to. My only refuge from this nightmare I was living in.

I really needed to talk to Jake and find out how he really felt about me. I needed to be reassured that he would stick by me even if I had to move. I was falling so hard! I called him and talked to him about how I felt toward him. I told him how much I loved him and asked if he felt the same.

He promised me we would get through all of this together. He told me he would stick by me no matter what happened. As I hung up the phone, my heart broke. I didn't want to let him go. I couldn't wait to get back home so I could see him again. I lay on the bed for hours and thought about all the sweet things he said. It was like music to my ears. He surprisingly understood me more than Tricia even did.

The weekend seemed so long. I couldn't wait to go home so I could see Tricia and Jake.

I talked to both of them on the phone quite a bit. I missed them, but I missed Jake more. My heart yearned to be around him every minute of the day. I think he felt the same.

Dad tried to bring me back to his world, but I now lived in my own little world. I was too preoccupied in my own mind to pay any real attention to what was going on around me. I talked and talked, and nobody heard me. Now I don't hear you either.

I still had no clue when we were moving and didn't really care to know. When I finally got home, I ran into my room, threw my stuff on my bed, and grabbed the phone. First call, Jake. The second call, Tricia. Mom came into the room just as I hung up the phone with Tricia.

"Well, Hello, Sam," she exclaimed as she held out her arms to hug me.

"Oh, hi," I replied politely.

"I missed you!" she said as she wrapped her arms around me.

"Missed you too, mom," I said as I made an effort to hug her back. I really had no feelings toward her at the moment, but I thought I better make an effort to at least act like I missed her.

She pulled me at arm's length and said, "Look at you, you're so pretty! I am so glad you're home." She gave me another hug and kissed me on the cheek.

"Thanks," I said, taken back by the compliment.

"Hey, it's been a while since I hung out with Tricia and Jake. Is it okay if they come over for a while?" I tried to be nonchalant.

"Uh…sure…" she said, acting kind of surprised. Normally, I would have wanted to spend my time with her, but not this time. I wanted to see the people who really cared about me.

Mom said, "But let's go chat over some cookies and milk before they come." Her eyes lit up as she proposed the idea.

"Nah," I replied. "I have to unpack before they get here." She didn't know I already called them and invited them over.

Mom's expression went from shining star to the walking dead in no time. I saw how disappointed she was, but I just didn't really care. I wanted to get my things put away before Tricia and Jake came over.

Jake got there first. He rode his bike over. I was so happy to see him. I miss him so much. As we stood in the yard, we could see Tricia and Tim riding their bikes down the street. We waved our arms frantically and hollered at them, just being silly. They were waving and hollering back.

We all ended up riding our bikes to the park. We messed around and talked about what happened at dad's house. The finality of me moving became so real to all of us. We all sat there in silence for a moment, just soaking it all in.

Tricia asked, "So what are you going to do?"

I shrugged, "Dunno." I thought about it for a bit, then finished, "I guess move."

Tricia looked down at her feet for a long time, then looked at me. She said, "This sucks so bad."

"I know," I acknowledged.

Jake put his arm around me and squeezed gently in support. I put my head on his shoulder, and my eyes welled up. I tried hard not to cry. It felt good to have these guys there for me. I just loved them! They were like my own family, but even better since my real family didn't support me at all.

The next few months of school, I grew closer and closer to Jake, Tricia and Tim. They were the only people I wanted to be around anymore. We would hitch a ride with Jake's older brother after school sometimes and go to the mall just to hang out together. Jake and I would hold hands as we walked through the mall. Tricia and Tim would too. They were getting pretty close.

These three people were now my world. We spent a lot of time riding bikes to the park and having picnics there. We all loved watching the people pass as we sat in the park. Some had dogs, and others were just strolling through. Some stopped at the playground to let their kids play for a bit. Others looked like they were on a mission with no time to waste. We would guess what kind of person each one would be and where they were heading. We did a lot of laughing as we slumped against the same old big tree each time and observed the people passing by.

With each day that went by, the realization of moving became closer. At the end of the school year, we were moving to Carl's. I started having anxiety attacks by the first week in May. I sooo didn't want to leave! My heart felt like it was being ripped out every time I thought about moving away from Jake, Tricia and Tim. It hurt to think I would be so far away from all three of them. They were my life now.

One day, Jake and I were riding our bikes in the park and I suddenly became overwhelmed with the thought of moving. The fear of never seeing him again crept up. I started crying and had to stop. I stood there in the middle of the bike path, bawling as I watched Jake ride ahead of me.

Jake finally noticed I stopped and came back for me.

"Hey, What's up?" he asked. Once he realized I was crying, he got off his bike and came over to hug me. "It's okay," he said as he pulled me close to him. I buried my face in his shoulder as he stroked my hair.

"I don't want to move," I said between the sobs.

"It's okay, don't worry, we'll still see each other," Jake spoke soothingly as he cupped my face in his hands. He looked deep into my tear filled eyes and said, "I'll have my brother drive me over every other day if I have to, okay?"

I let out a little giggle as I thought of his brother. He was such a goof. He would drive us wherever we wanted to go. We called him our taxi all the time. He went out and bought a hat with the word "taxi" on it. He always put it on every time we climbed into his car.

"You know he will. Besides, I will be getting my license in a few months," He said with some exaggeration.

"It's just scary," I said as I started to calm down.

"I love you, Sam. I won't forget you," he said as he kissed my tear-filled cheek.

That just made me feel like crying even more. I was so choked up I couldn't get out a word. We just stood there forever, just holding each other for the longest time.

On our ride home, I saw Carl's vehicle in the driveway. Anger suddenly filled me as I thought of what he was doing to my life and future. He was the one taking me away from all I knew.

I said goodbye to Jake and headed for the house. When I walked in I felt a certain prick in my heart. Mom and Carl were at the door. He held mom in his arms while she buried her face in his shoulder. I heard her say "I miss you already" as she looked up, and they both looked deep into each other's eyes.

That night, I wondered if mom and Carl were feeling the same thing I felt about Jake.

Mom kept telling me she was making a sacrifice for me to stay here for the school year. I always thought that was a lie, but now I wondered if maybe there was a little truth in that statement. If she felt anything close toward Carl as I felt toward Jake, it really would be a sacrifice.

All that night I tossed and turned, thinking about how hard it must be for her to wait until the school year to be over. I dreamt of mom and Carl in a house, living together happily. The dream was so vibrant, and there was so much love there. It just filled every void I ever had against those two. Yes, I thought as I lay there, feeling peace for the first time since mom and dad split up. Yes, mom, I understand now. Soon, mom would be happy and I would still get to keep my Jake. I smiled as I thought of Jake.

In the last six months, I have gained Lindy as a friend, Jake as my boyfriend, Tim as a friend, Carl as a soon-to-be stepdad, and two soon-to-be stepbrothers.

I thought of Taylor and Bradly being my stepbrothers for the first time. It hit me like a brick. I will finally have siblings. I always wanted a sister or brother.

I really needed to step up and be a part of the family. Besides, I am going to live in that big, beautiful dream home!

Yes, it was time to shed the anger and accept the changes in my life. It was time to find my own happiness. It was time to find my place in the family and truly fit in.

Life as I knew it would soon change, but somehow I knew in the end, everything really would be okay.

I smiled, closed my eyes and finally, I drifted off to a peaceful sleep.

www.ingramcontent.com/pod-product-compliance
Lightning Source LLC
Chambersburg PA
CBHW051202120626
46547CB00012B/1167